In Loving Memory

Of
Mary F. Lorelli
Mother
Of
Toni Manfredi
By
Blairsville-Saltsburg
School District

60 SIMPLE Clothing Crafts

for Making Wearable Art

Nancy Jo King

Lunchbox Press • Southlake, TX

ISBN 0-9678285-4-6

Copyright © 2002 Nancy King

Published by Lunchbox Press 701 Greymoor Place, Southlake, TX 76092.

Cover and interior design © TLC Graphics, www.TLCGraphics.com

Interior illustrations by Nancy Jo King

Photography by Lynne McCready

Printed in Canada

First printing, 2002

For all my Kings with a heart full of gratitude for your love: Geoff, Savannah, Ralph, Joel, Mandy, and Ethan.

Table of Contents

Body Gear

Footgear

Headgear

Table of Contents

Jewelry

Outergear

Fun and Fantasy

Accessories

Gifts

Resources

Introduction

Wouldn't it be cool to give your wardrobe a makeover? With these 60 easy-to-make crafts, you can add an artistic touch to anything in your closet — from hats to shoes and then some! You'll discover page after page of stylish ideas to let you show off your fashion flair. What makes it even better is all the fun you'll have creating these wearable works of art. So get ready to get crafty!

Why Get Crafty?

One of the best ways to express yourself is through art. It gives you a chance to flex your creative muscles, explore your artistic talent, and put your mind to work on something other than schoolwork! As an extra bonus, you wind up a really cool work of art that you made yourself. Besides, arts and crafts are just plain fun.

Getting the Gear

All of the materials needed to make the crafts in this book can be found at crafts or hobby stores; you might even have some of them at home already. If you can't find something, ask a sales associate to help you find the item or suggest a replacement. On page 83, you'll find a helpful list of national crafts stores and mail order catalogs.

Gold Star Muscle Tee

Stuff You Need

- "Muscle"-style sleeveless T-shirt
- 1 yard gold sequin trim (sold in fabric stores)
- Needle and thread
- Metallic gold fabric paint
- Paintbrush
- Pencil
- Cardstock or heavy paper to make pattern
- Scissors
- Paper plate
- Cardboard cut to fit inside T-shirt
- Newspaper to cover work area

You'll shine with this cute and easy-to-make tee!

What You Do

Use the star pattern on page 85, or create a heart design with cardstock. Fold the cardstock in half. Draw half of a heart from the fold and cut out.

Place the cardboard inside the T-shirt to prevent the paint from bleeding through, and to create a flat painting surface.

Place the pattern in the center of the front of the T-shirt and draw around it with the pencil.

Put a small amount of the metallic gold paint on a paper plate. Use the brush to apply the paint to your pattern. Take care to stay inside the outline. Let dry thoroughly before removing the cardboard.

Use the needle and thread to attach the gold sequin trim around the top front and back of the shirt. Use a simple running or hemstitch to sew (see sewing guide on page 84). Trim excess and your shirt is ready to wear!

Cute-As-A-Button Tee

Stuff You Need

- T-shirt
- "Puffy" fabric paint (sold in crafts or fabric stores)
- 12 assorted or matching buttons
- Needle and thread
- Scissors
- 5- by 5-inch piece of cardboard

Depending on the buttons you choose, this tee can be super simple or fairly fancy.

What You Do

Sew the buttons around the hem of one sleeve, spacing evenly apart.

Insert the 5- by 5-inch piece of cardboard into the sleeve of the T-shirt. This will prevent the paint from bleeding through the fabric as well as provide a flat surface to work on.

Use the "puffy" fabric paint to write "Cute As A" down the sleeve. Working in the center of the sleeve, begin the writing at the top and end near the hem. Let dry thoroughly.

. . . Or Try This

You can also sew buttons around the collar of the shirt for added pizzazz.

Potato-Printed Daisy Pants

Stuff You Need

- 1 pair of denim jeans
- White and yellow fabric paint
- Paper plate
- Paintbrush
- 1 large baking potato
- Pencil
- Plastic knife
- Newspaper to cover work area

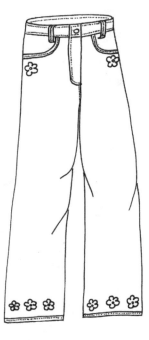

Use this simple printing technique to create one-of-a-kind designs!

What You Do

Cut the potato in half width-wise and use the pencil to trace or draw a simple flower design on it.

Use the plastic knife to cut around the design (about 1/4-inch deep).

Cut from the sides of the potato to the edge of the design to remove excess. This leaves the design "raised" for printing.

Pour a small amount of the white fabric paint on the paper plate. Dip the potato "stamper" in the paints. Blot once on another part of the paper plate, then press gently onto a selected area of your jeans. To prevent smearing, take care not to move the stamper while you're printing.

Repeat design as desired. Let dry thoroughly.

Pour a small amount of the yellow fabric paint onto another paper plate. Use the brush to paint a yellow circle in the center of each flower. Let dry and enjoy!

. . . Or Try This

You can make so many different designs with this super-simple printing technique. Make matching T-shirts, visors, or headscarves. You can add printed decoration to almost any fabric!

Pocket Garden Tee

Stuff You Need

- T-shirt with a pocket
- Green "puffy" fabric paint (available at fabric or crafts stores)
- Flower-shaped buttons or ribbon roses
- Needle and thread
- Cardboard to fit inside the T-shirt

Celebrate springtime year-round with this cheerful tee.

What You Do

Place the cardboard inside the T-shirt to prevent the paint from bleeding through to the other side, and to create a flat painting surface. Cut another small piece of cardboard to fit completely inside the pocket.

Use the pointed end of the "puffy" paint applicator bottle to draw flower stems coming up and out of the pocket. You may also want to add a few stems hanging over the top onto the front of the pocket itself. Add leaves as desired and let dry thoroughly.

Use the needle and thread to sew on the flower buttons or ribbon roses at the top of each stem.

. . . Or Try This

This technique is great for dressing up jean pockets, or for decorating an apron for someone special!

Stars and Stripes Tee

Stuff You Need

- White T-shirt
- Glitter fabric paint in red and blue
- Star stickers
- Flat-tipped paintbrush
- 1-inch wide masking tape
- Ruler
- Cardboard cut to fit inside T-shirt
- 8 1/2- by 11-inch piece of heavy paper
- Pencil
- Washable chalk
- Scissors
- Paper plate
- Newspaper to cover work area

Show your patriotic spirit with this cool T-shirt!

What You Do

Fold the paper in half. Starting from the folded edge, draw half of a large heart. Use the scissors to cut out the heart and unfold. This will be your pattern.

Place the cardboard inside the T-shirt to prevent the paint from bleeding through to the other side, and to create a flat painting surface.

Place the heart pattern in the center of the front of the T-shirt. Trace around it with the washable chalk. Use a ruler to mark off a square in the top left corner of the heart. Measure and mark off 1-inch wide stripes on the remainder of the heart. Put strips of masking tape on every other row, starting with the second row down.

Apply the star stickers in rows in the square of the heart. Press firmly on the edges of the stickers so you have good adhesion. Put a small amount of the blue glitter fabric paint on a paper plate. Brush the blue paint over the star stickers in the square, taking care to stay inside the chalk line. Let dry.

(continued on the next page)

Stars and Stripes Tee (cont.)

Put a small amount of the red paint on a paper plate. Paint each of the stripes without the masking tape on. When thoroughly dry, remove the masking tape and star stickers.

. . . Or Try This

For a different decorative effect, sew on small white star buttons instead of painting around the star stickers. Simply paint the square blue, let dry, then add buttons!

Fabric Crayon Transfer Tee

Stuff You Need

- T-shirt (white or light-colored works best)
- White drawing paper (or plain newsprint)
- Fabric crayons (available at crafts stores)
- Iron

Adult supervision required

Transferring designs with fabric crayons is a great way to show your creativity!

What You Do

On the white drawing paper (or plain newsprint), use the fabric crayons to color a picture or design you like. You'll have better results if you press hard with the fabric crayons, or go over each area of color more than once. Remember, if you want to include any writing, you will have to write "backwards," as the design will be reversed when transferred to the fabric.

Heat the iron to a cotton or linen setting. Place your crayon drawing face side down on the part of the T-shirt where you want it transferred. Press the iron over the back of the paper, making sure you iron all areas of the design. Take care that the paper does not shift or move during the transfer, or you will smear your design. You can check your transfer by gently lifting one corner of the paper. Gently lift off the paper to reveal your design. Allow the fabric to cool completely before handling.

(continued on the next page)

Fabric Crayon Transfer Tee (cont.)

... Or Try This

Using this great technique, you and your friends can each make a square of fabric designed with a crayon transfer, and then put together a cool quilt. Or, you can make book covers or napkins, or decorate your room! If you see a design you like but don't think you can draw it, use carbon paper to transfer it to your white paper, then fill in with the fabric crayons.

Careful! Ask an adult to help you use the iron.

Embossed Velvet-Cuffed Jeans

Stuff You Need

- Old pair of jeans
- Scissors
- Measuring tape or ruler
- 1/4 yard of velvet
- Needle and thread
- Straight pins
- Iron
- "Chunky" raised stamper

Adult supervision required

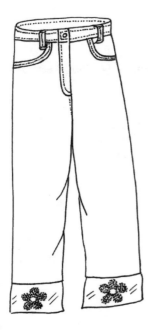

Add a touch of glamour to your jeans with beautiful and easy-to-make embossed velvet cuffs. This is a great project to recycle jeans you've grown too tall for.

What You Do

Cut off the bottom six inches of each jean leg. Trim off more if you want your finished jeans to be "capri" length.

Measure the diameter of the cut jean and add one inch. Cut two pieces of the velvet this measurement long by 7-inches wide.

Heat iron to a low setting. Place the chunky raised stamper with design facing up on the ironing board. Center the velvet face down over the stamper. Press the iron over the velvet, which will transfer and emboss the design onto the fabric. Reposition the velvet over the stamper and repeat as desired. Let fabric cool before handling.

Bring the two 7-inch right sides together and sew. Place the velvet cuff over the bottom of the jeans, with right sides facing together and pin the edges together. Sew this.

Hem the bottom of the cuffs and your new jeans are ready to wear!

Careful! Ask an adult to help you use the iron.

"Air Brushed" Stenciled Tee

Stuff You Need

- T-shirt
- Colorfast fabric paint in your favorite colors
- Spray bottles (one per color used)
- Plastic stencil in any design (available at crafts or fabric stores)
- Masking tape
- Cardboard to fit inside T-shirt
- Newspaper to cover work area

You don't need fancy equipment to get the look of an air brushed designer tee!

What You Do

Place the cardboard inside the T-shirt to prevent the paint from bleeding through to the other side, and to create a flat painting surface.

Center the stencil over the T-shirt, where desired, and use the masking tape to secure it to the shirt.

Fill the spray bottle with the desired color of fabric paint. Holding the bottle just a few inches above the stencil, pump the top of the bottle, releasing the paint onto the fabric.

Repeat the process, filling in the other areas of the design with the desired colors. Let dry thoroughly before removing the cardboard.

. . . Or Try This

Use leaves, cut-outs, or other imaginative objects as your stencil!

Silk Flower in My Pocket Tee

Stuff You Need

- T-shirt
- 5-inch square of sheer organdy fabric
- Ruler
- Pinking shears
- Straight pins
- Needle and thread
- Silk flower (a flatter one works best, such as a daisy or pansy)
- 1 yard of 1/4-inch wide satin ribbon

Dress up your tee by showing off a silk flower in a sheer pocket!

What You Do

Measure a 5-inch square out of the sheer organdy fabric. Cut out with pinking shears to give the edges a decorative finish.

Place the silk flower on the T-shirt where you want the "pocket" to be. Center the sheer organdy square over the flower. Use the straight pins to hold in place.

Outline the flower with the silk ribbon, leaving a 1/2-inch border all around the edges of the organdy, and pin in place.

Thread the needle and sew the silk ribbon in place, then remove the straight pins.

. . . Or Try This

You can show off any fun, washable object in a sheer pocket!

"Pointillism" Butterfly Shirt

Stuff You Need

- Shirt (can be a T-shirt, polo, or other pullover)
- Fabric paint in assorted colors
- Colored chalk
- Pencil eraser
- Paper plates
- Cardboard to fit inside the T-shirt
- Newspaper to cover work area
- White drawing paper
- Pencil
- Scissors

Pointillism is an art technique of applying small dots of color next to each other. Your eye will "mix" the colors when you view them from a distance. (For example, red and yellow placed together will visually blend into orange, blue and yellow make green, and red and blue make purple.)

What You Do

Fold the white drawing paper in half. Beginning at the top of the fold, draw half of a butterfly design. Use the scissors to cut out the design, then open the paper and you have your pattern.

Place the cut cardboard inside the T-shirt to prevent the paint from bleeding through to the other side, and to create a flat painting surface.

Center the pattern on your shirt. Trace around your pattern with the colored chalk.

(continued on the next page)

12

"Pointillism" Butterfly Shirt (cont.)

Put a small amount of different colors of paint onto a paper plate. Make your pointillism "dots" by dipping the pencil eraser in one color of paint, blotting once on the paper plate, then pressing the eraser onto a selected area of your pattern. Repeat until you have filled in all the areas you want to be that color. Wash and dry your pencil eraser and repeat with another color until your design is completely filled.

Let dry thoroughly before removing the cardboard.

Beaded Collar Tee

Stuff You Need

- T-shirt
- Approximately 320 seed beads or 240 pony beads (slightly larger)
- Needle and thread
- Ruler
- Colored chalk

This easy beading technique will add glamour to any clothing.

What You Do

Thread your needle with thread that matches the color of your T-shirt.

Begin in the center of the back of the collar. Use the ruler and chalk and mark off 1 inch spaces around the neckline of the T-shirt. (An average T-shirt collar measures approximately 16 inches but you can use any style pullover shirt.)

Starting at one of the chalk marks, bring the thread up from the wrong side to the right side of the T-shirt. Thread 15 pony beads (or 20 seed beads) onto the needle. Move them down the thread until the beads are up against the T-shirt fabric. Insert the needle back down into the next chalk mark, creating a "scallop" of beads.

(continued on the next page)

Beaded Collar Tee (cont.)

Bring the needle up right next to the same spot and repeat beading and sewing until you have circled the entire collar.

Crafting Hint: You will probably have to tie-off and re-thread your needle once or twice to finish this project. Simply tie your knots on the back side of the T-shirt neckline.

. . . Or Try This

You can add a scalloped edge of beading to the hem of your short sleeves, shirt hem, or jean cuffs. Or try adding a personal touch to a pillowcase hem as a special gift!

Mini Sarong

Stuff You Need

- 1 yard tropical print rayon fabric
- 2 yards 1-inch wide satin ribbon
- Measuring tape
- Scissors
- Straight pins
- Needle and thread in a color that coordinates with fabric

You can make this fun skirt for summer parties or as a cute swimsuit cover-up.

What You Do

Measure around your waist and add half of this measurement to your total. For example, if your waist measures 24 inches add another 12 inches for a total of 36 inches. This will be the width of your skirt.

Measure from your waist to just above your knees. This measurement will be the length of your skirt. Cut out a rectangle of the rayon fabric using these measurements.

To make the ties, pin the satin ribbon along the top edge (long end) of the fabric, leaving 12 inches of ribbon loose on one end and 24 inches on the other end (to wrap around). Sew the ribbon to the skirt.

Sew a hem around the other three edges of the fabric. To wear, simply wrap the skirt around your waist, overlap the front and tie together. You may want to cut a small slit through the ribbon at the side to hold it in place where it ties.

Lace Stenciled Jeans

Stuff You Need

- Pair of jeans
- White fabric paint
- Flat-tipped stencil brush
- Paper doilies (can be round, rectangular, or square — but pick ones with pretty designs and lots of cut-outs)
- Scissors
- Masking tape
- Paper plate
- Newspaper to cover work area

Dress up your jeans with this fun stencil technique!

What You Do

Cut out a piece of the doily design you want to use. You will want a section at least 2- or 3-inches wide and as long as your paper doily.

Place the paper doily on your jeans where you want your painted stencil. (A good place might be just above the hem of the pants.) Tape down the ends of the doily with the masking tape to hold it in place.

Place some of the white fabric paint onto the paper plate. Holding your stencil brush at a 90 degree angle (upright) to the plate, press the brush into the paint and blot once on the paper plate.

(continued on the next page)

Lace Stenciled Jeans (cont.)

Gently press the loaded brush onto the stencil. The paint will pass through the holes in the doily, but not through the other parts, leaving a painted impression of the lace stencil on your jeans.

Carefully lift the stencil from your jeans. Give that area a few minutes for the paint to "set" before you begin another section. Cut a new piece of paper doily, align it to your previously painted areas, and repeat stencil painting around your jeans until you have achieved your desired effect.

Rhinestone Name Tee

Stuff You Need

- "Muscle" style T-shirt
- Clear or colored rhinestones
- Washable fabric glue (available at crafts or fabric stores)
- Tweezers
- Paper plate
- Washable colored chalk
- Cardboard cut to fit inside the T-shirt

You and your friends can all make matching T-shirts with this cool idea!

What You Do

Place the cardboard inside the T-shirt. This will prevent the glue from bleeding onto the other side.

Use the washable chalk to write your name (or other desired word) centered on the front of the T-shirt.

Pour a small amount of the washable fabric glue onto a paper plate. To attach the rhinestones, use the tweezers to pick up a stone, then gently dip the back side in the glue. Place it on the shirt over the writing, pressing for a moment to let it set.

Repeat until you have covered your name with rhinestones. Let dry thoroughly.

. . . Or Try This

It may be easier if you make a name stencil on the computer. Simply select a font style you like, then spell out your name in the size you want it to be, and print. If using a white T-shirt, place the printed stencil under the shirt where it will show through and use the chalk to trace over the letters.

Sequined Thongs

Stuff You Need

- 1 pair thong-style flip flops
- White "tacky" glue
- Scissors
- 1 yard sequin trim (sold in fabric stores)
- Ruler

Why buy fancy designer thongs when you can make your own as easy as one-two-three?

What You Do

Measure the top of the thong straps with the ruler. Use the scissors to cut the sequin trim into four pieces, each measuring 1 inch longer than the thong strap.

Run a line of the "tacky" glue along the top of each thong strap. Fold over each end of the sequin trim a 1/2 inch and add another drop of glue under the edge of the fold. Press the sequin strip onto the top of each thong strap where you have applied the glue.

Let dry thoroughly. You may want to hold the trim in place with small pieces of masking or blue painter's tape if it starts to slide while it is drying.

. . . Or Try This

Thongs can be decorated with almost any material or ribbon. Try a woven ribbon, and add a button, silk flower, or other ornament to the center of the thong.

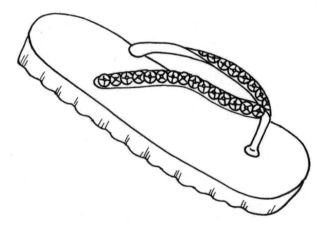

Tie-Dye Socks

Stuff You Need

- Pair of white cotton socks
- Permanent markers
- 20 rubber bands
- Rubbing alcohol in a spray bottle
- Iron
- Newspaper to cover work area

Adult supervision required

Here's a great technique to get the look of tie-dye without the mess.

What You Do

Loop the rubber bands tightly around each sock, about 2 inches apart.

Push the tip of a permanent marker onto each sock at different places, leaving some of the sock white. Let the marker tip rest in the fabric for a minute so the sock can soak up some of the ink. You can use one color, or achieve a rainbow effect by using lots of different colors.

Spray the rubbing alcohol onto the socks and watch the colors bleed together. Let dry for about two hours before you remove the rubber bands.

Cover the socks with a damp cloth and iron. This will set the colors. (The socks should be washed in cold water.)

Careful! Ask an adult to help you with the iron.

Daisy Slip-Ons

Stuff You Need

- 1 pair slip-on style shoes
- 1/4 yard white vinyl fabric
- 2 yellow buttons
- Scissors
- Pencil
- Needle and thread
- White paper
- Carbon paper

Why wear plain old slip-ons when you can decorate them with funky leather-look daisies?!

What You Do

Place the carbon paper and the white paper under the daisy pattern. Trace and cut out.

Transfer the pattern to the white vinyl fabric. Trace and cut two daisies from the vinyl.

Position the daisy on the top of the shoe. Sew the yellow button onto the center of the daisy by bringing the knotted thread up from the inside of the shoe, through the daisy, up through the button hole, and then back down through the daisy and the shoe. Repeat sewing until the daisy is firmly attached, and knot the thread underneath the daisy.

Repeat with the second shoe.

Beaded Socks

Stuff You Need

- Pair of socks
- Needle and thread (in a color that matches socks)
- 144 small white pony beads
- 12 6mm crystal beads
- Scissors
- Ruler
- Chalk

Turn an ordinary pair of socks into extraordinary footgear!

What You Do

Use the ruler and chalk and mark off 1-inch spaces around the top edge of the socks (an average sock will have a diameter of approximately 6 inches).

Thread your needle with thread that matches the color of your socks.

Starting at a chalk mark, bring up the needle from the side of the sock that will be underneath the cuff when the top of the sock is folded over. Thread six small white pony beads onto the needle, add one of the 6mm crystal beads, and follow with six more small white pony beads. Insert the needle back down into the top of the sock at the next chalk mark. This will create a looped "scallop" of beads.

Bring the needle up right next to the same spot and repeat the beading pattern until you have circled the entire top of the sock. Tie and knot your thread when finished.

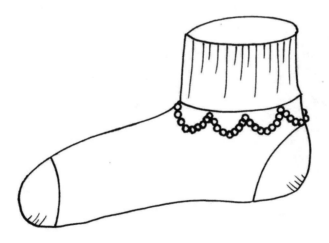

Buttons and Bows Socks

Stuff You Need

- Pair of socks
- 12 decorative buttons (stars, hearts, etc.)
- 12 1-inch ribbon bows (available in fabric stores)
- Needle and thread (in a color that coordinates with socks)

With so many cool buttons available now in crafts and fabric stores, the possibilities are limitless! Coordinate patterns and colors with a favorite outfit.

What You Do

Fold over the cuff of the sock and decide on a desired pattern. You may want to sew your buttons and bows in a neat row around the edge of the cuff, or be more abstract and freestyle.

Place a ribbon bow on the sock. Use the threaded needle and attach the bow to the sock with a few tacking stitches. Place a button over the center of the ribbon bow and sew it in place.

Repeat sewing on the buttons and ribbon bows until you have the desired pattern. Knot your thread after the last button is attached, and trim off excess thread.

Apply the ribbon bows, and buttons to the other sock to match.

Beaded Shoelaces

Stuff You Need

- 1 pair of shoelaces
- Polymer clay in desired colors
- Straw
- Dozen clear or colored 8mm round plastic beads

Adult supervision required

Show off your creativity with decorative beaded shoelaces.

What You Do

Select one or more color of polymer clay. Divide it into 1/4-inch pieces. Roll each piece of clay between the palms of your hands to create a ball. Use the straw to poke a hole through the ball. Make four beads per shoelace.

Bake the clay beads according to the manufacturer's directions.

Tie a knot about 4 inches from the end of each shoelace. Add one 8mm round plastic bead.

Follow this with a clay bead. Alternate the plastic and clay beads, ending with a plastic bead. Knot the shoelace again to hold the beads in place.

Crafting Hint: This craft must be made while shoelaces are in shoes.

(continued on the next page)

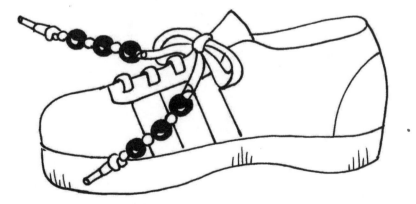

Beaded Shoelaces (cont.)

. . . Or Try This

If desired, you can use self-hardening clay for this project. For a funky look, try marbling your clay. Simply "mush" two colors together and then roll them into a ball (make sure you don't completely blend the colors or you will just create a new solid color!).

Careful! Ask an adult to help you use the oven.

Flower Power Flip Flops

Stuff You Need

- 1 pair of thong sandals
- "Tacky" glue or hot glue gun
- 2 silk daisies
- Daisy "chunky" stamp (available in crafts or fabric stores)
- Acrylic paint in a coordinating color
- Paintbrush
- Newspaper to cover work area

Adult supervision required

These cool summer thongs are as fun to make as they are to wear.

What You Do

Place a bead of glue in the center top of the thong straps. (To make "tacky" glue, add 1 teaspoon of cornstarch to white glue.) Place one daisy flower into the glue. Hold the daisy in place for a few minutes to allow it to set.

Brush the acrylic paint onto the top surface of the daisy chunky stamp. Carefully turn the stamp over and press onto the top of the foot platform of the thong. Apply gentle pressure and take care not to let the stamper move. Repeat stamping design, if desired (especially if using a smaller design). Let dry.

. . . Or Try This

This idea can be adapted to any theme. Try ribbon roses, buttons, jewels, or rhinestones.

Careful! Ask an adult to help you use the hot glue gun.

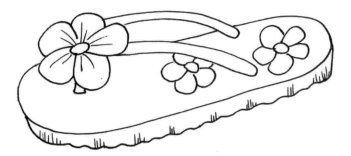

Heart Stenciled Visor

Stuff You Need

- Visor (can be plastic or fabric) in a light color
- Red or pink fabric paint
- Hole punch
- Plastic lid (like the lid of a potato chip can)
- Paper plate
- Flat-tipped stencil brush
- Red rhinestones
- Index card or small piece of paper
- Pencil
- Scissors
- Glue
- Masking tape
- Newspaper to cover work area

You'll look cool under cover when you wear this artistic visor!

What You Do

Fold the index card or small piece of paper in half. Use the pencil to draw half of a heart from the folded edge and cut out. The heart must be small enough to fit inside the plastic lid.

Place the heart pattern inside the plastic lid and trace around it. Punch holes around the design, leaving a small space between each hole. This will be your stencil. (You can cut off the rim of the plastic lid, if needed.)

Center the lid on the top of your visor brim and tape in place. Pour a small amount of red or pink paint onto the paper plate. Holding your stencil brush upright at a 90 degree angle to the paint, dip it into the paint. Blot once on the paper plate, then gently press the brush onto the stencil.

(continued on the next page)

Heart Stenciled Visor (cont.)

Take care not to let the stencil move, or you will smear your design. Repeat until your pattern is transferred to your visor. Let dry.

Glue red rhinestones around the band part of your visor. Let dry.

. . . Or Try This

You can adapt this idea to any theme. Try stars in silver paint with silver rhinestones glued on.

Woven Ribbon Headband

Stuff You Need

- 14-inch length of 1-inch wide striped woven ribbon
- 6-inch length of 1/4-inch wide elastic
- Scissors
- Ruler
- Needle and thread
- 2 straight pins

Keep your hair in place with this simple-to-make headband!

What You Do

Fold the ends of the woven ribbon and pin each to one end of the elastic (stretch the elastic to fit the length of ribbon).

Sew the ribbon and elastic together. Remove pins and enjoy your new headband!

. . . Or Try This

If you have extra ribbon, make a cool matching choker necklace by tying a 12-inch piece around your neck. You can also pin on an old cameo or other decorative jewelry.

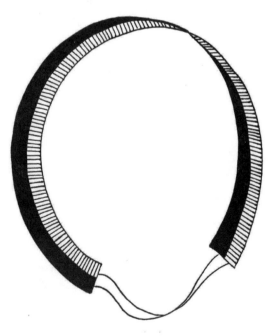

Beaded Chopsticks Hair Ornament

Stuff You Need

- 1 pair wooden chopsticks
- Black acrylic or craft paint
- Paintbrush
- Straw
- Small clear and colored rhinestones
- Gloss decoupage glue
- Polymer clay in desired colors
- Newspaper to cover work area

Adult supervision required

For that exotic look, you'll love these easy-to-make hair sticks!

What You Do

Paint the wooden chopsticks black. Let dry thoroughly.

Select two colors of polymer clay. To "marble" the clay, pinch off about 2 inches of each color and form two coils by rolling clay on a hard surface with the palm of your hand. Roll the two coils together and gently "mush" them until the colors begin to blend together. Don't overdo the mixing or they will become one new color!

Break off small sections of marbled clay and roll into 1/4-inch balls. Make a hole in the center of each by gently pressing, then twirling the end of the straw into the ball. You can slide the bead down to where you want it on the chopstick, so the opening in the bead will be the right size.

(continued on the next page)

Beaded Chopsticks Hair Ornament (cont.)

Remove from the chopstick and bake according to the manufacturer's directions.

Slide the baked clay beads to the last 2 inches of the fatter end of the chopsticks. Paint the chopsticks with the gloss decoupage glue. While glue is wet, add rhinestones as desired. Let dry. Style your hair by sliding the smaller, undecorated ends into your bun or twist.

Careful! Ask an adult to help you use the oven.

"Leather" Hair Slide

Stuff You Need

- Vinyl "leather-look" fabric scrap
- Scissors
- Hole punch
- Pencil
- Paintbrush
- Acrylic paints in desired colors
- Paper plate
- Bamboo skewer stick
- Newspaper to cover work area

Give your ponytail a little pizzazz with this "leather" slide.

What You Do

Draw a 5-inch oval on the vinyl fabric scrap and cut out.

Punch a hole 1/2 inch from the edge of each short side.

Place a small amount of desired paint colors onto a paper plate. Paint miniature flowers or other decorative shapes around the edges of the vinyl oval. Let dry thoroughly.

Paint the stick a coordinating color. Let dry thoroughly.

To wear, simply gather hair into a ponytail. Place the hair slide over the ponytail and insert the stick in one of the holes, under the ponytail, and up through the other hole, letting some of the stick extend out each end.

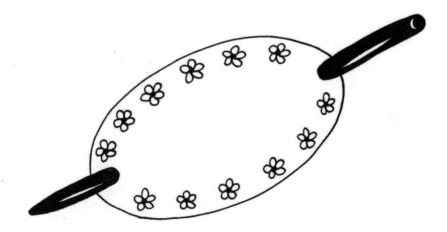

Fleece Headband

Stuff You Need

- 1/2 yard fleece fabric
- Scissors
- Washable chalk
- Ruler
- Straight pins
- Needle and thread (in a color that coordinates with the fleece)

Since fleece doesn't require hemming, this headband is a snap to make.

What You Do

Measure out two rectangles of fleece 7 inches long by 2 inches wide. Mark with the washable chalk and cut out. Measure, mark, and cut out another rectangle 11 inches long by 4 inches wide.

Thread the needle and sew a loose running stitch 1/4 inch from each end of the 4-inch wide edge of the larger piece of fleece. Do not knot the thread; leave a few inches of thread hanging at each end. Gently pull the thread to gather the fleece to a width of 2 inches.

Pin this gathered end, right sides together, to one of each of the smaller rectangles of fleece. Sew together using smaller stitches, and knot the ends of your thread to secure. Trim off extra thread and your new headband is ready to wear. Simply wrap around your head and tie the ends together at the nape of your neck.

Running Stitch

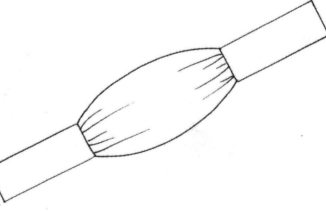

Rhinestone Bandana

Stuff You Need

- Bandana in any color
- Fabric glue (sold in fabric or crafts stores)
- Rhinestones in assorted colors
- Tweezers

Rhinestones are the rage, and what better way to shine than by dressing up an ordinary bandana?

What You Do

Lay your bandana out on a flat surface. You can accent a pattern by outlining it with rhinestones, or just add rhinestones randomly throughout the design. Wherever you want a rhinestone, simply add a dot of fabric glue, then pick up the desired colored rhinestone with the tweezers and place it into the glue. Press gently with the other end of the tweezers to help it set.

Repeat adding rhinestones as desired. Let the glue dry completely before picking up or moving the bandana.

. . . Or Try This

Purchase a 1/2 yard of fabric in a cool print, like something Hawaiian, surfer style, or floral. Cut fabric into an 18-inch square, and hem all the edges. Add rhinestones to accent the design.

Boa Trimmed Baseball Cap

Stuff You Need

- Baseball cap
- Scissors
- 24-inch long feather boa
- White craft or fabric glue
- Wax paper to cover work area

Dress up your favorite baseball cap with a crown of boa feathers.

What You Do

Cut the feather boa to 24 inches in length.

Run a line of white glue around the crown of the baseball cap. Wrap the feather boa around the cap, gently pressing it into the glue. Hold in place a few minutes while the glue sets. Trim off excess feather boa.

Let the cap dry on the wax paper to catch any drips.

. . . Or Try This

Add even more style to your baseball cap with a pin-on silk flower, buttons, ribbon roses, or other decorations!

Origami Hair Ornament

Stuff You Need

- 1 pair wooden chopsticks
- Scrap of sandpaper
- Scissors
- Printed origami or other decorative paper
- Glue stick
- Paper plate
- Acrylic paint
- Paintbrush
- Newspaper to cover work area

This super-simple craft makes a beautiful hair accessory!

What You Do

Break apart the wooden chopsticks. Smooth off any rough edges with the sandpaper. Pour a small amount of acrylic paint onto the paper plate. Paint the sticks and let dry thoroughly.

Cut the origami or other printed paper into a 4- by 1 1/2-inch rectangle.

Apply the glue stick generously to the last 4 inches of the wider end of the chopstick. Wrap the paper around the chopstick, adding more glue as it overlaps. Press the edges and hold to secure while the glue sets. Let dry thoroughly.

Style your hair by sliding the undecorated ends into your bun or twist and the sticks will hold your hair in place!

Woven Mini Belt Bracelet

Stuff You Need

- 8-inch length of 1-inch wide striped woven grosgrain ribbon
- 2 1-inch wide "D" rings (sold in fabric stores)
- Needle and thread (or sewing machine)
- Scissors
- Straight pins

Adult supervision required

Be on top of the latest trend with this cool woven bracelet!

What You Do

Cut an 8-inch length of 1-inch wide grosgrain ribbon. Double fold one end 1/4 inch to make a hem, then pin and sew. (To double fold, fold over 1/4 inch, then fold it over again another 1/4 inch.) Use a sewing machine or hem by hand with a simple running stitch. Remove the straight pin.

On the other end, fold over 1/4 inch and run the ribbon through the flat part of both of the "D" rings. Pin the ribbon down just below the "D" rings, and sew the ribbon together. Remove the straight pin.

To put the bracelet on, wrap the ribbon around your wrist. Loop the end through both of the "D" rings, then bring the end back through just one of the "D" rings, like a belt buckle. Tighten to desired length and enjoy!

(continued on the next page)

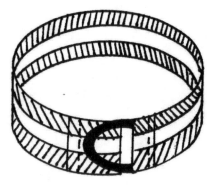

Woven Mini Belt Bracelet (cont.)

. . . Or Try This

Mini belt bracelets are so quick and easy you can create several in matching colors and patterns to wear together! They also make great gifts for your friends.

Careful! Ask an adult to help you use the sewing machine.

Mini Tussie-Mussie Flower Pin

Stuff You Need

- Real, dried, or silk rose or other flower
- Sprig of dried baby's breath
- 8-inch piece of 1/2-inch wide ribbon
- Scissors
- Green floral tape
- 8-inch paper doily
- Pin back (sold in crafts or fabric stores)
- White glue

A "tussie-mussie" is a special holder for flowers, and it originated in Victorian times. These mini flower pins are perfect for gift-giving!

What You Do

Cut the stem of the flower to three inches.

Add some of the baby's breath around the flower. Wrap the flower and baby's breath together with the green floral tape.

Fold and cut the paper doily in half and then half again so you have 1/4 of the doily. Place this behind the flower and gather the middle around the arrangement. Tie in place with an 8-inch piece of ribbon and tie it into a bow.

Glue a pin back onto the back side of the tussie-mussie. Let dry thoroughly before trying it on.

. . . Or Try This

You can make tussie-mussie place cards or party favors and tuck a little card with the name of your guest inside each one. Try adding a sprig of rosemary or other herb for added fragrance.

Silk Flower Pin

Stuff You Need

- Silk flower
- Pin back (sold in crafts or fabric stores)
- White glue or hot glue gun
- Waxed paper to cover work area

Adult supervision required

Here's a unique accessory that's super-simple to make!

What You Do

Remove the stem from the flower so you have a nice, flat base to work with.

The glue gun works best for this project, but requires adult supervision. If you need to you can substitute white glue. Apply glue to the back of the flower and attach it to the pin back. Hold in place while the glue sets.

You can wear your silk flower as a decorative pin, or attach it to a baseball cap, hair "scrunchie," or backpack.

. . . Or Try This

Try using several small flowers to decorate a barrette. Simply arrange and then glue on.

Careful! Ask an adult to help you use the hot glue gun.

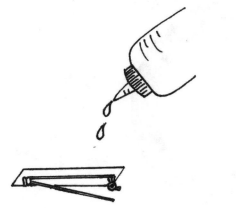

Painted Bangle Bracelet

Stuff You Need

- Plain wooden bangle bracelet
- Acrylic or craft paints
- Gloss decoupage glue
- Paintbrush
- Paper plate
- Paper or plastic cup
- Newspaper to cover work area

Create a coordinating accessory to match your favorite outfit with this easy craft!

What You Do

Put small amounts of paint onto the paper plate. Paint desired design or motif onto your wooden bangle bracelet. Place the bracelet over an upside down paper or plastic cup to hold it while it dries thoroughly.

Paint a coat of clear gloss finish decoupage glue over the painted bangle to protect the design. Let dry thoroughly.

. . . Or Try This

For an even cooler look, you can decoupage your bangle bracelet. Cut out small paper designs such as flowers or stars. After painting the entire bangle, let dry, and brush on the gloss decoupage glue. Attach pieces of the cut-out paper designs, one at a time, pressing out any air bubbles with the brush. Apply another coat of decoupage glue to the top of the paper. Let dry.

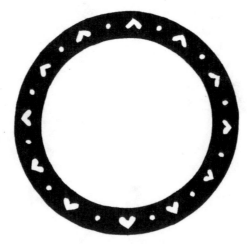

Striped Heart Necklace

Stuff You Need

- Red, white, and pink polymer clay
- Rolling pin
- Plastic knife
- Straw
- Thin ribbon, cut 16 inches in length

Adult supervision required

This easy necklace makes a great accessory, as well as a simple-to-make gift!

What You Do

To make a "striped" slab of clay you'll need about five different-colored coils. Roll the clay on a flat surface, and then use the palm of your hand to apply gentle pressure to form a long, tubular shape.

Place each coil very closely together on a flat surface. With the rolling pin, gently roll the clay into a 1/4-inch slab.

With the plastic knife or toothpick, draw and cut out a heart shape from the clay (see heart-shaped pattern on page 85). Make a hole near the top center of the heart with the straw.

(continued on the next page)

Striped Heart Necklace (cont.)

Bake the clay according to the manufacturer's directions, or air dry if using self-hardening clay.

Thread the heart onto the ribbon. Tie it around your neck.

... Or Try This

Best friends can make matching necklaces by making a slightly larger heart, cutting it in half, and poking a hole in the top of each half.

Careful! Ask an adult to help you use the oven.

Beaded Safety Pin Cuff Bracelet

Stuff You Need

- 30 safety pins (1-inch pins work great)
- 60 6mm beads in one color
- 120 4mm beads in same or other desired colors
- Elastic cord
- Needle
- Scissors
- Ruler
- Clipboard

You can make awesome jewelry with just safety pins and a few beads!

What You Do

Decide on what color pattern you want your cuff bracelet to be. You can use beads of all one color, alternate colors, or mix random colors. Open each safety pin and thread four 4mm beads onto the open part. Close the pin.

Measure and cut two pieces of elastic cord to 8-inch lengths.

Tie a knot in one end of one piece of elastic and clip the knot under the clamp part of a clipboard to hold in place while you work. Thread the elastic cord onto a needle and alternately add one beaded safety pin, then add one 6mm bead. Repeat until you have filled 6 inches of the elastic cord. This will take approximately 30 safety pins and 30 of the 6mm beads. Tie and knot the end of the piece of elastic cord to keep the beads and pins from falling off the cord.

Thread another piece of elastic cord through the hole at the top of each safety pin, adding another 6mm bead between each pin. Repeat until you have connected the other end of each safety pin. Tie each end of elastic together, knot securely, and trim off excess. Stretch the bracelet over your wrist and enjoy!

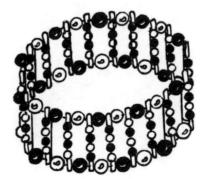

Sea Glass Necklace

Stuff You Need

- Jewelry wire
- Clasp
- 2 crimper beads
- Scissors
- Needle nose pliers
- 84 6mm clear crystal beads
- Beach glass (available in crafts stores)

Turn beautiful sea-washed beach glass into a one-of-a-kind necklace.

What You Do

Cut a 6-inch piece of the thin jewelry wire. Wrap it around the beach glass like you are tying up a package. Leave enough wire at the top of the beach glass to create a loop, using the needle nose pliers.

Cut a piece of thin jewelry wire to a 20-inch length. Add a crimper bead to one end, then loop the end through one part of the clasp, and back down through the crimper bead. Pull tight and use the needle nose pliers to squeeze the crimper bead to flatten it and secure the clasp.

(continued on the next page)

Sea Glass Necklace (cont.)

Starting from the opposite end of the jewelry wire, begin threading the clear crystal beads onto the wire. Stop when you have strung half of the beads. Attach the wired beach glass to the necklace by threading it through the loop.

Continue adding the remainder of the crystal beads. Add the second crimper bead, loop the wire through the other part of the clasp and back through the crimper bead. Use the needle nose pliers to squeeze the crimper bead to flatten it and secure the clasp.

Braided Hemp Ankle Bracelet

Stuff You Need

- 1 1/2 yards of hemp cord
- Scissors
- Ruler
- 10 to 12 colored "E" beads
- Paper clip
- Clipboard

Try wearing several of these braided and beaded hemp ankle bracelets.

What You Do

Measure and cut the hemp cord into three 16-inch lengths. Knot the three pieces together about 3 inches from one end. Clip the knotted end of the cord under the clamp of a clipboard to hold in place while you work.

Braid the three pieces of hemp cord, adding a colored bead every 1/2 inch or so. Place a paperclip on the braid when adding the bead to keep the braid from unraveling.

Continue braiding and beading until you have filled 9 inches. Tie and knot the cord, leaving about 3 inches.

Wrap around your ankle and tie the ends together.

Beaded Barrette

Stuff You Need

- Flat metal barrette
- 30-gauge seed beads (approximately 75 per barrette, depending on width)
- Spool wire
- Scissors
- Needle nose pliers

A few beads can turn an ordinary barrette into an extraordinary hair accessory!

What You Do

Open the barrette. Cut a 24-inch length of wire from the spool. Wrap one end twice around the top of the barrette, near the hinge. Catch the end under several pieces of wrapped wire on the underside on the barrette to secure.

Bringing the wire up to the top of the barrette, add three seed beads. Slide the beads down the wire until they rest on the top of the barrette. Wrap the wire around the back of the barrette.

Each time you bring the wire up to the top, add three more beads. Repeat beading and wrapping until the entire top of the barrette is covered.

Cut the wire about 2 inches past the last bead. Slip this end under several of the pieces of wrapped wire on the underside of the barrette.

Suede Bracelet

Stuff You Need

- 2 pieces of different colored suede (sold in crafts stores in 9- by 3 3/4-inch strips)
- Hole punch
- Scissors
- Pencil
- Ruler
- Needle and thread (in a color that coordinates with suede)
- 2-inch piece of Velcro

Leather cuffs are a popular accessory, and you can make your own suede bracelet with this easy craft!

What You Do

Measure and cut two strips of suede, each 2 1/2 inches wide by 6 inches long. (Craft suede is very soft and will cut easily with scissors.)

Use a pencil to mark your design on one strip of suede. Following your pencil marks, punch holes in the suede with the hole punch.

Place the piece of suede with the punched holes over the other piece of suede, with both pieces sueded side up. Sew the shorter ends together.

Sew one piece of the Velcro on each end of the cuff bracelet, one on the top of one end, and one on the bottom side of the other end. Wrap around your wrist and close with the Velcro.

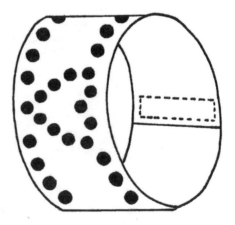

Ankle Bracelet

Stuff You Need

- 10-inch piece of elastic string
- Needle
- 80 pony beads in desired colors
- Scissors
- Clipboard

Ankle bracelets are cool to wear and to give as gifts.

What You Do

Cut a 10-inch length of elastic string and thread the elastic onto the needle.

Knot one end and place it under the clamp part of a clipboard to hold it in place and prevent the beads from slipping off while you work.

Thread 80 pony beads onto the needle and elastic string. This will fill about 8 inches of the elastic, leaving the other 2 inches for tying and knotting. You can alternate colors or use random colors to create a pattern.

(continued on the next page)

Ankle Bracelet (cont.)

When the beading is complete, take the end of the elastic out from under the clipboard, tie both ends together, and knot securely. Your ankle bracelet will now stretch to fit over your foot and onto your ankle.

. . . Or Try This

Try making several ankle bracelets in coordinating colors and wear them together!

Paper Bead Necklace

Stuff You Need

- Origami or other decorative paper
- 12 6 to 8mm round silver or colored beads
- White glue
- Scissors
- Pencil
- Elastic string
- Needle
- 3 to 5 cotter pins (found in hardware or crafts stores — or you can use toothpicks if cotter pins are unavailable)
- Wax paper to cover work area

This necklace looks so awesome, your friends won't believe it's made of paper.

What You Do

Use the pattern shown here, or make your own by cutting a triangle that is 1 inch across the flat edge, and 6 inches down each side. (For a fatter bead, make your triangle 8 inches long.) Cut out about twelve triangles for each choker style necklace.

(continued on the next page)

Paper Bead Necklace (cont.)

To roll a paper bead, slightly open a cotter pin and insert the flat 1-inch part of the paper, aligning it with the cotter pin. Begin rolling the paper around the pin, keeping it centered. When you are at the last inch, apply a small amount of white glue onto the paper. Roll this last part of the bead, pressing and holding it for a moment. Set aside on the wax paper to dry. After the glue has set and sealed the edges of the paper (this will only take a few moments) gently slide the bead off the cotter pin.

Repeat with the other paper triangles until you have made the desired number of beads.

Cut a 16-inch length of the elastic string and thread it onto the needle. Wrap the other end around one of the cotter pins to keep the beads from sliding off while stringing. Alternate stringing a bead, then a paper bead, onto the elastic until you have filled the elastic. Remove the cotter pin and securely tie and knot the ends. The necklace will easily stretch to fit over your head.

Button Toe Rings

Stuff You Need

- Pipe cleaner
- Scissors
- Ruler
- Button in a flower or other design (with sewing loop on the bottom of the button)

Show off your pedicure with these adorable toe rings.

What You Do

Cut the pipe cleaner to 4 1/4 inches. Wrap it around the toe you will be wearing the ring on for correct size and twist the two ends together once.

Put one of the pipe cleaner ends through the loop on the bottom of the button. Twist together once more and tuck the ends of the pipe cleaner under the button.

. . . Or Try This

Colored vinyl-covered wire (such as "Twisteez" brand sold in crafts stores) is fun to work with and makes great jewelry. Cut a piece long enough to go around your toe, adding enough on both ends so that you can loop and twist it into a pretty design.

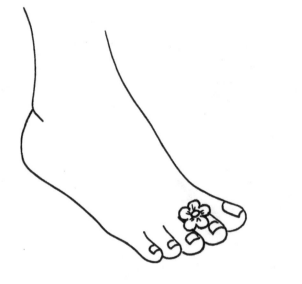

Medals Ribbon

Stuff You Need

- 30-inch length of woven striped ribbon
- Scissors
- 2-inch diameter drinking glass or cup
- Pen
- Craft foam in any color
- Paper plate
- Tweezers
- Approximately 30 sequins in desired color
- White craft glue
- Hole punch
- Newspaper to cover work area

Showcase all your coolest buttons, pins, or medals on this special ribbon!

What You Do

Cut the ribbon to a 30-inch length.

Use a glass or other round object with a 2-inch diameter as your circle pattern. Place the glass over the white craft foam and draw around it. Cut out the circle. Punch a hole in the circle about 1/2 inch from the edge.

Write your initials on the foam circle. Pour a small amount of the glue onto a paper plate. Use the tweezers to pick up a sequin, dip it in the glue, and press gently onto the writing on the foam circle. Repeat until both of the initials are outlined in sequins.

Thread the foam circle and center it onto the ribbon. Attach your pins, buttons, or medals to the ribbon and enjoy!

Beaded Hair Wrap

Stuff You Need

- 1 bobby pin
- Assorted beads: jet, round, crystal diamond, or 4mm pearls
- 1 drop bead
- 12-inch piece of clear cord for beading
- 2 crimper beads
- Needle nose pliers

Add sparkle to your tresses with this easy-to-make beaded hair wrap!

What You Do

Add one crimper bead to one end of the clear cord. Loop the cord through the round end of the bobby pin and back through the crimper bead. Slide the crimper bead as close to the bobby pin as you can and use the needle nose pliers to squeeze the crimper bead shut.

Thread the beads onto the cord in desired pattern. Near the end add another crimper bead, then loop the cord through the hole in the drop bead and bring the cord back up through the crimper bead. Hide the end in the other beads near the end. Use the needle nose pliers again to squeeze and tighten the crimper bead.

Attach one or more of your hair wraps where desired by pinning it underneath some of your hair to hide the bobby pin.

Barrette Pockets

Stuff You Need

- Metal "spring" barrette clip
- Felt scrap
- White glue
- Needle and thread
- Pinking shears
- Pencil

Dress up those plain metal barrettes with these cute felt "pockets."

What You Do

Place the barrette over 2 stacked pieces of felt and use the pencil to draw around it, adding 1/4 inch all around.

Use the pinking shears to cut out your pattern. You will now have two matching pieces.

Put some white glue on one of the pieces of felt, place the top part of the barrette between the two pieces of felt, and press together.

Use the needle and thread to sew around the outside edges of the barrette, leaving the pinking sheared edges as a decorative trim. Let dry thoroughly before using.

. . . Or Try This

For a dressier barrette, add rhinestones, beads, or sequins to the top piece of felt.

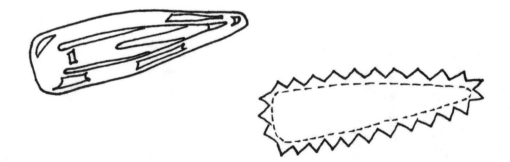

Rain Poncho

Stuff You Need

- 1 1/2 yards of glossy vinyl fabric
- Scissors
- "Puffy" paint in desired colors
- Paper plate
- Measuring tape
- Pen

Keep warm and dry in this easy-to-make poncho!

What You Do

Spread the fabric on a flat surface. Measure and mark a circle with a 48-inch diameter. Cut out.

Measure and mark another 8-inch circle in the center for the head opening. Cut out the circle and add a small 4-inch slit at the front (as shown).

Try on your poncho and mark two 8-inch lines in the front sides for your arms to fit through. Remove poncho and cut slits.

Decide on a design or motif for the border of your poncho. Draw your design with the puffy paint. You may want to practice a little on the paper plate to get the feel of using the puffy paint. Let dry thoroughly.

Fun Fur Mittens

Stuff You Need

- 1/4 yard fake fur
- 2 knit cuffs
- Needle and thread
- Straight pins
- White paper
- Carbon paper
- Pencil
- Scissors

Keep your hands toasty this winter with these furry mittens.

What You Do

Make a pattern of your hand by placing one hand on a piece of white paper. Don't spread your fingers but let your thumb rest naturally to the side. Draw around your entire hand, adding 1 inch all around. Repeat and cut out both patterns.

Fold the fur in half, right sides together. Place one of the patterns on the "wrong" side of the fake fur. Pin in place and cut out the two pieces for the first mitten. Unpin the pattern, turn it over and place it again on the "wrong" side of the remaining fake fur. Pin in place and cut out the two pieces for the other mitten.

Pin the two matching sides of the mittens, fur part facing each other, together and sew around the outside, leaving the wrist open. Repeat with the other two cut pieces.

Pin the knit cuff to the wrist part of the mitten, laying right sides together. Sew together. Remove the pins, turn mittens inside out, fold the cuffs back down, and your mittens area ready to wear!

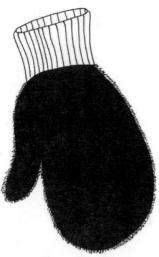

Fleece Scarf

Stuff You Need

- 1/3 yard of fleece fabric in desired color
- Scissors
- 12 buttons
- Needle and thread in a color that coordinates with fleece

This super-simple scarf makes a great winter gift for a loved one.

What You Do

Cut out a rectangle 12-inches wide by the length of the fabric.

Starting 1 1/2 inch in from each shorter end (the one which measures 12 inches), sew on buttons spaced two inches apart. Repeat until you have sewn six buttons on each end.

Fold the edge under 1 inch and sew a hem on each end for a nice, clean finish.

. . . Or Try This

Add some fringe to the ends of the scarf by making 2-inch deep cuts, spacing them about 1/2 inch apart. The fleece will not unravel or need hemming.

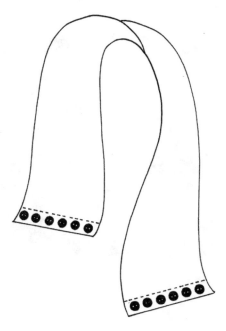

Silver Beaded Tiara

Stuff You Need

- Four silver pipe cleaners (12 inches long)
- 32 silver beads (8mm)
- Scissors

Let your inner princess out with this beaded tiara!

What You Do

Overlap the ends of two of the pipe cleaners about an inch and twist together. Form a circle, overlap the remaining ends of the pipe cleaners about an inch, and twist them together to form a head ring.

Measure and cut one of the remaining two pipe cleaners in half, creating two pieces of equal length. Thread eight of the silver beads onto one of the cut pipe cleaners. Move the beads to the center of the pipe cleaner. Repeat with the remaining cut pipe cleaner.

(continued on the next page)

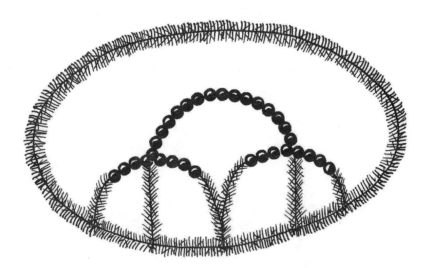

Silver Beaded Tiara (cont.)

Bend one of the beaded pipe cleaners to form a half circle. Loop and twist the ends onto the large pipe cleaner ring. Repeat and attach the second beaded pipe cleaner directly beside the first looped and beaded pipe cleaner. Twisting the ends tightly will secure them in an upright position from the head ring.

Use the scissors to trim the last pipe cleaner to 10 inches long. Thread 16 of the silver beads onto the pipe cleaner and center. Bend the pipe cleaner into a 1/2 circle. Attach this third beaded pipe cleaner to the head ring by placing one end in the center in front of one of the smaller beaded 1/2 circles and the other end centered in the back side of the second 1/2 circle. Twist the ends tightly onto the head ring.

Crafting Hint: Beads will slide on more easily if you put them on the uncut end of the pipe cleaner.

Rock Star Glasses

Stuff You Need

- Heavy cardstock or poster board
- Markers
- Feathers
- Star stickers
- Glitter
- Rhinestones
- Colored cellophane
- Glue
- Tape
- Scissors
- Newspaper to cover work area

Get into the groove with these fun-to-make glasses!

What You Do

Using pattern shown, cut one glasses frame and two ear pieces from heavy cardstock or poster board. Attach the ear pieces to the glasses by taping securely in place.

Cut pieces of cellophane large enough to cover the eye openings. Glue or tape onto the back of frame.

Use markers to decorate frames. Add glitter, rhinestones, star stickers, and glue on feathers. Let dry.

(look at the next page for the pattern)

Rock Star Glasses (cont.)

Hawaiian Lei

Stuff You Need

- 40 silk tropical flowers (such as hibiscus)
- 80 8mm beads in clear or matching colors
- Elastic cord
- Tapestry needle (large needle with a dull point)
- Scissors
- Ruler or tape measure

These festive necklaces make the perfect party favor for a Hawaiian-themed bash!

What You Do

Measure and cut a piece of elastic cord to a 30-inch length. Thread the elastic cord onto the tapestry needle.

Remove the stems from the flowers, so you have the loose petals.

Begin threading the lei by alternating two layers of petals with two beads. Repeat until you have filled the lei. Finish by tying a knot in the elastic cord and trimming the excess.

. . . Or Try This

You can substitute 1-inch pieces of cut clear or colored straws in place of the beads.

Beaded Sunglasses Strap

Stuff You Need

- Two plastic eyeglass holders (available at crafts or drugstores)
- 24-inch long clear plastic cord
- 80 6mm beads in desired colors

Be cool this summer with a handmade beaded strap for your shades!

What You Do

Thread one end of the clear plastic cord onto one of the eyeglass holders. Tie a knot, leaving about 1/2 inch of plastic cording. The knot will be hidden by the first few beads.

Choose a desired pattern for your beading, alternating colors, or stringing them randomly for a rainbow effect. Thread the beads onto the plastic cord, sliding them all the way down. Continue adding beads until you have about two inches of cord left.

Add the other eyeglass holder on the end of the cord, tie and knot. Hide the end of the cord by pushing it inside the beads.

Attach to your sunglasses and enjoy!

Handkerchief Drawstring Bag

Stuff You Need

- 2 matching handkerchiefs or bandanas
- 1 yard seam binding
- 1 yard 1/4-inch wide satin ribbon
- Straight pins
- Safety pin
- Scissors
- Needle and thread*

Optional: You can do the sewing for this project on a machine with adult supervision, if desired.

Make a dressy purse from a handkerchief or create a contemporary bag using bright bandanas.

What You Do

Pin the two handkerchiefs together, right sides facing each other. Thread the needle with a coordinating color of thread and sew three of the edges together.

Carefully turn the purse inside out. Pin the seam binding two inches from the open edge, going all the way around the purse. Carefully sew the top and bottom edge of the seam binding to the purse, leaving a 1-inch open space.

(continued on the next page)

Handkerchief Drawstring Bag (cont.)

Clip the safety pin onto the edge of the yard of satin ribbon. Using the safety pin as a "handle," guide the ribbon through the open space of the seam binding, and work it through the length of the seam binding. Bring the safety pin and ribbon through the open space again when you have gone all the way around the purse. Remove the safety pin. Tie the ends of the ribbon together and knot.

Close the purse by pulling gently on the ribbon ends and open it by gently pulling on the gathers.

Careful! If you're using a sewing machine, ask an adult to help you.

Ring-Handled Purse

Stuff You Need

- 1/4 yard fabric
- Two wooden or plastic rings six inches in diameter (available in fabric stores)
- Needle and thread in a color that coordinates with fabric
- Scissors
- Straight pins

Keep all your stuff handy with this easy-to-make purse.

What You Do

Cut a rectangle of fabric 8-inches wide by 18-inches long. Fold it in half with right sides facing each other. With the fold at the bottom, pin the two sides together.

Thread the needle and sew the two sides together, leaving the top 2 inches open on each side. Remove the straight pins and turn the fabric inside out to hide the side seams.

Fold over the top hem 1/4 inch. Place the wooden (or plastic) rings, one on each side of the top and fold over the fabric around the ring. Pin in place and then sew. Remove pins and push the fabric together to gently gather on the ring handles.

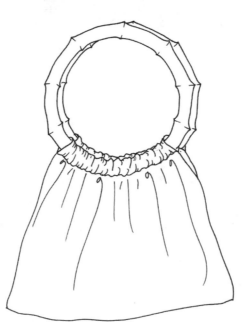

Jean Pocket Purse

Stuff You Need

- Old pair of jeans or denim shorts
- Washable chalk
- Scissors
- Straight pins
- Needle
- 30-inch length of clear plastic cord (or fishing line)
- 120 6mm colored beads

Don't throw away those old jeans — make an awesome fringed pocket purse!

What You Do

Use the washable chalk to draw around a back pocket on an old pair of jeans, leaving another 3 inches of denim under the pocket. Use the scissors and cut out.

Cut the extra denim under the pocket into 1/4-inch strips to make the fringe.

Thread the plastic cord onto the needle. Attach to one side of the top of the jean pocket and knot securely. Thread the beads onto the cord, leaving about 3 inches at the end of the clear cord. Sew and knot this other end to the opposite side of the jean pocket purse to make your shoulder strap. Enjoy!

(continued on the next page)

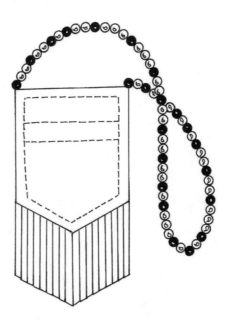

Jean Pocket Purse (cont.)

... Or Try This

Lace and knot pony beads onto your fringe for added decoration. You can also add iron-on appliqués to the pocket, or try cutting designs out of printed fabric and applying them with iron-on fusible interfacing!

Earring Holder

Stuff You Need

- 6- by 6-inch piece of pink or red craft foam
- 8-inch piece of fishing line or other cord
- Nail
- Hammer
- Scissors
- Pencil
- Ruler
- Newspaper to cover work area

Adult supervision required

Keep your earrings tidy and organized with this handy holder!

What You Do

Use the pencil to trace or draw a 6-inch heart on the craft foam and cut out.

Starting from the bottom center of the heart and 1/8 inch from the edge, use the ruler to mark off pencil dots every 1/2 inch going up around the sides of the heart. Stop before you reach the curve at the top of each side of the heart. Make one hole at top center of the heart for the hanger.

Use the hammer and nail to make holes where each pencil dot is. Simply hold the nail over the pencil dot, and hammer gently until it pokes through the craft foam. Working on several folded pieces of newspaper will provide a good surface to nail upon.

Careful! Ask an adult to help you use a hammer.

Earring Holder (cont.)

Loop the fishing line or other cord through the hole at the top of the heart and knot to secure it.

... Or Try This

You can make hearts in lots of different colors if you have a lot of earrings. They'll look great hanging together.

Personalized Key Chain

Stuff You Need

- Polymer clay in at least two different colors
- Plastic knife or toothpick
- Straw
- Rolling pin
- Ball chain key chain

Adult supervision required

Keep track of your keys with this super-simple key chain, personalized so you always know it's yours!

What You Do

Start with a 2-inch ball of any color polymer clay. With the rolling pin, gently roll the clay into a medium-thick slab (about 1/4 inch).

With the plastic knife or toothpick, cut out a rectangle approximately 2- by 3-inches.

Select a 3-inch ball of another color of clay. Roll out long, thin coils. Work on a flat surface, and use the palm of your hand to apply gentle, rolling pressure to form a long, tubular shape.

(continued on the next page)

Personalized Key Chain (cont.)

Use the coils to write out your initials. One-inch tall letters take a 3- to 4-inch coil. You can try writing your whole name if it doesn't have too many letters and you make your letters a little smaller.

Form each letter and lay it onto your rectangle, pressing the letters in gently. Twirl the straw into the center of the short end of the rectangle to make a hole. When hardened, insert ball chain through the hole.

For extra strength, bake your clay according to manufacturer's directions.

Crafting Hint: You can use a ruler to measure and mark your lines for a perfect rectangle.

. . . Or Try This

These name tags also make cool IDs for backpacks, lockers, or the door of your room!

Careful! Ask an adult to help you use the oven.

Stamped Umbrella

Stuff You Need

- Solid color umbrella
- "Chunky" stamps in floral or other desired motif
- Fabric paint in selected colors
- Paper plates
- Paintbrush
- Newspaper to cover work area

You'll have it made in the shade with this hand-stamped umbrella!

What You Do

Open the umbrella and place on the newspaper covered work area. Put a small amount of each of the selected colors of fabric paint on paper plates.

Dip paintbrush in desired color of paint and apply to the raised design on the chunky stamp. Gently press the painted side of the stamp onto the umbrella, taking care not to let it move or you will smear the design. It may be helpful to position the umbrella over the corner of a table, so you will have a support underneath where you are pressing.

Repeat design as desired around the umbrella. Let dry thoroughly before closing the umbrella.

"Quilted" Heart Apron

Stuff You Need

- Solid color apron
- 1/4 yard fusible interfacing
- Assorted fabric scraps
- Scissors
- Straight pins
- 8 1/2 x 11 inch paper
- Pencil
- Ruler
- Needle and thread
- Puffy paint in a coordinating color
- Iron

Adult supervision required

This craft makes a great gift for a special someone.

What You Do

Fold the paper in half, and draw half of an 8-inch heart along the fold. Cut out the heart and unfold the paper.

Cut the assorted fabric scraps into 64 1-inch squares. Cut out an 8-inch square of the fusible interfacing. Arrange the fabric squares over the interfacing, with the "bonding" side up. The squares should slightly touch each other on each side.

Heat iron on a high setting and fuse the squares to the interfacing, following the manufacturer's directions on the interfacing. Let cool. Place the paper heart pattern over the fused fabric and cut out a heart from this fabric.

(continued on the next page)

"Quilted" Heart Apron (cont.)

Place the fabric heart on the apron, pin in place, then sew around the edges.

Decorate the outside of the heart with a border of the puffy paint.

. . . Or Try This

You can use this great technique on T-shirts or almost any piece of clothing.

Careful! Ask an adult to help you use the iron.

Painted Hands Apron

Stuff You Need

- Solid color "chef's style" apron
- Fabric paint in desired colors
- Paintbrush
- Paper plates
- Newspaper to cover work area

This project makes a great gift for that special teacher, mom, or grandmother.

What You Do

Lay the apron out on a flat surface.

Put a desired color of paint onto a paper plate. Dip paintbrush into paint, and paint the entire palm and fingers of your hand (the one not holding the brush!). This is a fun craft to do with a friend, as you can take turns painting each other's hands!

Press the painted hand onto the apron, taking care not to smear your hand. Lift gently and see the painted impression left behind.

Repeat printing the painted hands as desired.

(continued on the next page)

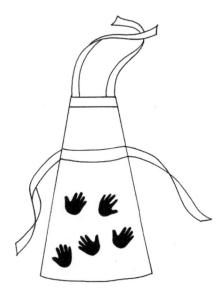

Painted Hands Apron (cont.)

. . . Or Try This

For a great classroom gift, each student can make his or her hand impression on the apron and write their name in puffy paint underneath their handprint.

Where to Shop . . .

The following is a list of craft and fabric retailers and catalogs where you can find supplies mentioned in this book:

Retail Outlets

A.C. Moore
www.acmoore.com

Garden Ridge
www.gardenridge.com
1-888-621-3814

Hancock Fabrics
www.hancockfabrics.com

Jo-Ann Fabrics and Crafts
www.joann.com
1-888-739-4120

Michaels
www.michaels.com
1-800-642-4235

Mail Order

Discount School Supply
www.earlychildhood.com
1-800-627-2829

Nasco Arts & Crafts
www.enasco.com
1-800-558-9595

S & S Education
1-800-243-9232

Sax Arts & Crafts
www.artsupplies.com
1-800-558-6696

Sewing Guide

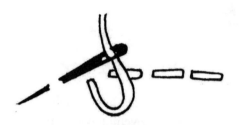

Running (hem) Stitch

Back Stitch

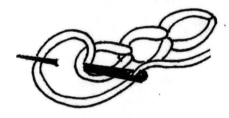

Chain Stitch

Design Ideas

Many of the projects in this book feature hearts, flowers, stars, and other shapes and designs. To help you get started, we've included a few traceable patterns you can use to decorate your wearable art.

Acknowledgments

Thanks to Brad, Lynne, Debbie, Marcella, and Kelly for your friendship; to Lori and Nancy from Lunchbox Press for your support; and Momma and Joy Talley for your inspiration.

About the Author

Nancy Jo King has been a professional artist and teacher for over 15 years. Her work has been featured in exhibits nationwide, including the National Association of Art Educators' annual convention. She has a passion for children's arts, and has been a craft designer for young adult magazines such as *Smackers* and *All About You*. King taught at the elementary level for many years, and has written, developed, and facilitated a curriculum for K-6 visual arts education. She lives in Southern California with her son and daughter. Nancy is also the author of *Get Crafty: 60 Cool Holiday Crafts for Year-Round Fun*.

Christmas, Halloween, Hannukah, Fourth of July — all are here with tons of great ideas for unique crafts you can create yourself to celebrate each occasion. From unique jewelry and ornaments to hand-made gift wrap and stationery, *Get Crafty* is chock-full of cool projects for you, your friends, and your family to try. So roll up your sleeves and get ready to "Get Crafty"!

Yes! I want to Get Crafty with 60 Cool Holiday Crafts for Year-Round Fun!

Please send _____ copy(ies) at $7.95 each plus $3 postage and handling for the first book and $1.50 for each additional. (Texas residents add 7.25% tax.)

TOTAL: _____

Name_____

Address _____

City _____ State _____ Zip _____

Phone _____

E-mail _____

Charge my: ☐ VISA ☐ MC ☐ AmEx or   ☐ Check enclosed

Card # _____

Exp. _____ Signature _____

Return payment to: Lunchbox Press, 701 Greymoor Place, Southlake, TX 76092 or call toll-free 866-776-2223

PUBLISHED BY LUNCHBOX PRESS
FALL 2001, ISBN 0-9678285-3-8

CLASSIC TREASURY

CLASSIC TALES

Miles Kelly

First published in 2015 by Miles Kelly Publishing Ltd
Harding's Barn, Bardfield End Green, Thaxted, Essex, CM6 3PX, UK

Copyright © Miles Kelly Publishing Ltd 2015

2 4 6 8 10 9 7 5 3 1

Publishing Director Belinda Gallagher

Creative Director Jo Cowan

Editorial Director Rosie Neave

Design Manager Joe Jones

Production Elizabeth Collins, Caroline Kelly

Reprographics Stephan Davis, Jennifer Cozens, Thom Allaway

ISBN 978-1-78209-819-5

Printed in China

British Library Cataloguing-in-Publication Data
A catalogue record for this book is available from the British Library

ACKNOWLEDGEMENTS
The publishers would like to thank the following artists
who have contributed to this book:
Cover
Main image: Cosei Kawa at Advocate Art
Other elements: Alice Brisland at The Bright Agency, LenLis/Shutterstock.com,
kusuriuri/Shutterstock.com, Lana L/Shutterstock.com, Markovka/Shutterstock.com
Inside pages
Cosei Kawa (Advocate Art), Jan Lewis, Ayesha Lopez (Advocate Art),
Kristina Swarner (The Bright Agency), Milena Jahier, Laura Wood

Made with paper from a sustainable forest

www.mileskelly.net
info@mileskelly.net

CONTENTS

ALONE IN THE WORLD

NEW FRIENDS

SECRETS REVEALED

SAVING THE DAY

MUCH MISCHIEF

ABOUT THE AUTHORS

Learn more about some of the famous authors behind these much-loved stories.

Louisa May Alcott
1832–1888

Little Women is Alcott's most famous book. She began it in the hope it might pay off some of her family's debts. In it, she told stories from her own childhood with her sisters May, Elizabeth and Anna. It was an enormous success and she became both wealthy and an unwilling celebrity.

'Christmas Wishes' from *Little Women*

Anna Sewell
1820–1878

Lamed in an accident when she was fourteen, Sewell often travelled by carriage, and hated the cruel treatment of the horses. She wrote *Black Beauty* in response to this, saying its special aim was "to induce sympathy, kindness and an understanding treatment of horses".

'Ginger' and 'A Stormy Day' from *Black Beauty*

About the Authors

Lewis Carroll
1832–1898

Carroll spent his adult life at Oxford University in the UK, teaching and studying mathematics and logic. He invented the story that would later become *Alice's Adventures in Wonderland* while out on a boat trip with the three daughters of a friend – Lorina, Edith and Alice Liddell.

'Down the Rabbit-hole' and 'A Mad Tea-party' from *Alice's Adventures in Wonderland* • 'Wool and Water' from *Through the Looking-glass*

Frances Hodgson Burnett
1849–1924

Burnett's childhood was one of poverty – an experience that she would later include in some of her novels. In 1865 her family moved from Manchester in England to Tennessee in the United States, where she began to earn money writing for magazines. She went on to write more than forty books.

'Sara' and 'A French Lesson' from *A Little Princess* • 'The Key to the Garden' and 'The Robin who Showed the Way' from *The Secret Garden*

About the Authors

L. Frank Baum
1856–1919

Lyman Frank Baum hated his first name and preferred to be called Frank. His greatest success was *The Wonderful Wizard of Oz*, and he went on to write thirteen books about the magical land of Oz, and many other short stories, poems and scripts.

'The Journey Begins' from *The Wonderful Wizard of Oz*

Susan Coolidge
1835–1905

Coolidge was interested in writing from a young age, and turned to it as a career after working as a nurse during the American Civil War. Her own family – Susan herself, her three younger sisters, her brother and her cousin – were the inspiration for the Carr family in *What Katy Did*, and the four books in the series that followed.

'The Little Carrs' from *What Katy Did*

About the Authors

Kenneth Grahame
1859–1932

Grahame's mother died when he was five, and he and his siblings were raised by their grandmother. Unable to afford to go to university, he took a job in the Bank of England. Grahame began to write about the characters that would later appear in *The Wind in the Willows* in letters to his son.

'The Riverbank' and 'The Wild Wood' from *The Wind in the Willows*

E Nesbit
1858–1924

Nesbit used the initial 'E' rather than her full name, 'Edith', to disguise the fact that she was a woman. She wrote more than forty books for children, and created the idea of mixing real-life characters and settings with magical elements.

'The Terrible Secret' and 'Saviours of the Train' from *The Railway Children*
'Golden Guineas' from *Five Children and It*

ABOUT THE ARTISTS

Milena Jahier Born in Argentina, Milena grew up in England and Mexico before moving to Italy to study illustration at the European Institute of Design. Since then she has worked on designs for packaging, products and logos, as well as illustrating greeting cards, murals and books. She works traditionally, using mixed media on paper.
Sara • A French Lesson

Cosei Kawa Since finishing his MA in Illustration at University College Falmouth in the UK, Cosei has illustrated numerous children's books. He uses a variety of mediums including acrylic, watercolour, collage, and digital effects to create work that is both naïve and detailed. He lives in Kyoto, Japan where he also teaches illustration at Kyoto University of Art and Design, and enjoys meditation, reading and music.
Cover • The Key to the Garden • The Robin Who Showed the Way

Jan Lewis Based in Oxfordshire in the UK, Jan has been working as an illustrator since 1978. She has produced work for many publishers, as well as BBC children's television. Since gaining her MA in Authorial Illustration Jan has enjoyed writing and illustrating her own books for children.
The Riverbank • The Wild Wood • A Mad Tea-party • Wool and Water

About the Artists

Ayesha Lopez As a small child, Ayesha loved to draw – unluckily for her parents this meant drawing on their furniture. Now she combines paper and computer to produce her charming, quirky illustrations. She lives in London in the UK.
The Caravan Siege • Two Visits and What Came of Them • Christmas Wishes

Kristina Swarner Magical and dreamlike, Kristina's work draws much of its imagery and inspiration from memories of exploring old houses, woods and gardens when she was a child. She lives in Chicago, USA, where she illustrates all kinds of things from books, greeting cards and magazines to wine labels and theatre posters.
Ginger • A Stormy Day • Pollyanna and Punishments • The Little Carrs • The Banquet Lamp

Laura Wood Growing up in the north of Italy, Laura devoured books and drew on the kitchen walls of her parents' house. She is now a full-time illustrator of picture books, educational publications and digital apps, among other things. She lives between Bristol, Melbourne and Milan, and she especially loves the process of finding the right colour palette, and bumping into funny (and furry!) characters in amusing stories.
The Journey Begins • The Terrible Secret • Saviours of the Train • Golden Guineas

ALONE IN THE WORLD

Sara

From *A Little Princess*
by Frances Hodgson Burnett

Once on a dark winter's day, when the yellow fog hung so thick and heavy in the streets of London that the lamps were lighted and the shop windows blazed with gas as they do at night, a little girl sat in a cab with her father and was driven rather slowly through the big thoroughfares.

She sat with her feet tucked under her, leaning against her father, who held her in his arm as she stared out of the window at the passing people with an old-fashioned thoughtfulness in her big eyes.

Sara

"Papa," she said in a low, mysterious little voice which was almost a whisper, "papa".

"What is it, darling?" Captain Crewe answered, holding her closer and looking down into her face.

"Is this the place?" Sara whispered, cuddling still closer to him. "Is it, papa?"

"Yes, little Sara, it is. We have reached it at last."

And though she was only seven years old, she knew that he felt sad when he said it. It seemed to her many years since he had begun to prepare her mind for 'the place', as she always called it. Her mother had died when she was born. Her young, handsome, rich, doting father seemed to be the only relation she had in the world. She only knew he was rich because she had heard people say so. She had always lived in a beautiful bungalow, and had been used to seeing many servants who let her have her own way in everything. She had learnt that people who were rich had these things.

During her short life only one thing had

troubled her, and that thing was 'the place' she was to be taken to some day. She had seen other children go away to school, and had known that she would be obliged to go also, and she had been troubled by the thought that her father could not stay with her.

"Couldn't you go to that place with me, papa?" she had asked when she was five years old. "I would help you with your lessons."

"But you will not have to stay for long, Sara," he always said. "There will be a lot of little girls, and you will play together, and you will grow so fast that it will seem scarcely a year before you are big and clever enough to come back and take care of papa."

"Well, papa" she said softly, "if we are here I suppose we must be resigned."

He laughed at her old-fashioned speech and kissed her. He was not resigned himself, though he knew he must keep that a secret. His little Sara had been a great companion to him, and he felt he should be lonely when, on his return to India, he went into his house knowing he need not expect to see the small figure come to meet him. So he held her in his arms as the cab rolled into the square in which stood the house which was their destination.

It was a big, dull, brick house, and when they got close to the door they could see there shone a brass plate on which was engraved in black letters:

MISS MINCHIN,
SELECT SEMINARY FOR YOUNG LADIES

"Here we are, Sara" said Captain Crewe, making his voice sound as cheerful as possible. Sara often thought afterwards that the house was somehow exactly like Miss Minchin. It was respectable and well furnished, but everything in it was ugly. The drawing room into which they were ushered was covered by a carpet with a square pattern upon it, the chairs were square, and a heavy marble timepiece stood upon the heavy marble mantel.

As she sat down in one of the chairs, Sara cast one of her quick looks about her. "I don't like it, papa," she said. "But then I dare say soldiers – even brave ones – don't really like going into battle."

Captain Crewe laughed outright at this. He never tired of hearing Sara's queer speeches. "Oh, little Sara," he said. "What shall I do when I have no one to say solemn things to me?" And then suddenly he swept her into his arms and kissed her, looking almost as if tears had come into his eyes.

It was just then that Miss Minchin entered the room. She had large, cold, fishy eyes, and a large, cold, fishy smile. It spread itself into a very large smile when she saw Sara and Captain Crewe. She had heard a great many desirable things of the young soldier from the lady who had recommended her school to him. Among other things, she had heard that he was a rich father who was willing to spend a great deal of money on his little daughter.

"It will be a great privilege to have charge of such a beautiful, promising child, Captain Crewe," she said, taking Sara's hand. "Lady Meredith has told me of her cleverness. A clever child is a great treasure in an establishment like mine."

Sara stood quietly, with her eyes fixed upon Miss Minchin's face. 'Why does she say I am a beautiful child?' she was thinking. 'I am not beautiful at all. Colonel Grange's little girl, Isobel, is beautiful. She has dimples and rose-coloured cheeks, and long hair the colour of gold. I have black hair and green eyes; besides which, I am a thin child and not fair in the least. I am one of the ugliest children I ever saw. She is beginning by telling a story.'

She was mistaken, however, in thinking she was

an ugly child. She was not in the least like Isobel Grange, who had been the beauty of the regiment, but she had an odd charm of her own. She was a slim, supple creature, rather tall for her age, and had an intense, attractive little face. Her hair was heavy and quite black and only curled at the tips; her eyes were greenish grey, it is true, but they were big, wonderful eyes with long, black lashes, and though she herself did not like the colour of them, many other people did. Still she was very firm in her belief that she was an ugly little girl, and she was not at all elated by Miss Minchin's flattery.

After she had known Miss Minchin longer she learnt that she said the same thing to each papa and mamma who brought a child to her school.

Sara stood near her father and listened while he and Miss Minchin talked. She had been brought to the seminary because Lady Meredith's two little girls had been educated there, and Captain Crewe had a great respect for Lady Meredith's experience.

Sara

Sara was to be what was known as a 'parlour boarder', and she was to enjoy greater privileges than parlour boarders usually did. She was to have a bedroom and sitting room of her own; she was to have a pony and a carriage, and a maid to take the place of the ayah who had been her nurse in India.

"I am not in the least anxious about her education," Captain Crewe said with a light laugh, as he held Sara's hand and patted it. "She is always sitting with her little nose burrowing into books, and she wants grown-up books – great, big, fat ones – French and German as well as English – history and biography and poets, and all sorts of things. Drag her away from her books when she reads too much. Make her ride her pony or go out and buy a new doll. She ought to play more with dolls."

"Papa," said Sara, "if I went out and bought a new doll every day I should have more than I could be fond of. Emily is going to be my intimate friend."

Captain Crewe looked at Miss Minchin and

Miss Minchin looked at Captain Crewe.

"Who is Emily?" she inquired.

Sara's green-grey eyes looked very solemn and quite soft as she answered.

"She is a doll I haven't got yet," she said. "We are going out together to find her. I have called her Emily. She is going to be my friend when papa is gone. I want her to talk to about him."

Miss Minchin's fishy smile became very flattering indeed. "What an original child!" she said.

"Yes," said Captain Crewe, drawing Sara close. "She is a darling little creature. Take great care of her for me, Miss Minchin."

Sara stayed with her father at his hotel until he sailed away again to India. They went out and visited many shops together, and bought a great many things. They bought, indeed, a great many more things than Sara needed, but Captain Crewe wanted his little girl to have everything she admired and everything he admired himself, so between them they collected a wardrobe much too grand for a child of seven. There were velvet dresses, and lace dresses, and embroidered ones, and hats with great ostrich feathers, and ermine coats, and boxes of gloves and handkerchiefs and silk stockings in such abundant supplies that the polite young women behind the counters whispered to each other that the little girl must be at least some foreign princess.

And at last they found Emily, but they went to a number of toy shops and looked at a great many dolls before they discovered her.

"I want her to look as if she wasn't a doll really," Sara said. "I want her to look as if she listens when I talk to her." So they looked at big ones and little ones, at dolls with black eyes and dolls with blue, at dolls with brown curls and dolls with golden braids.

After a number of disappointments they decided to walk and look in at the shop windows and let the cab follow them. They had passed two or three places without even going in, when, as they were approaching a shop which was really not a very large one, Sara suddenly clutched her father's arm. "Oh, papa!" she cried. "There is Emily!"

A flush had risen to her face and there was an expression in her green-grey eyes as if she had just recognized someone she was fond of.

"She is actually waiting there for us!" she said. "Let us go in to her."

"Dear me," said Captain Crewe, "I feel as if we ought to have someone to introduce us."

"You must introduce me and I will introduce you," said Sara. "I knew her the minute I saw her."

She had certainly a very intelligent expression in her eyes when Sara took her in her arms. She was a large doll, but not too large to carry about easily. She had naturally curling golden-brown hair, and her eyes were a deep, grey-blue, with thick eyelashes that were real eyelashes and not mere painted lines.

"Of course," said Sara, looking into her face as she held her on her knee, "papa, this is Emily."

So Emily was bought and actually taken to a children's outfitter's shop and measured for a wardrobe as grand as Sara's own. She had lace frocks, too, and velvet and muslin ones, and hats and coats and beautiful lace-trimmed underclothes, as well as gloves and handkerchiefs and furs.

"I should like her to look as if she was a child with a good mother," said Sara. "I'm her mother, though I am going to make a companion of her."

Captain Crewe would really have enjoyed the shopping tremendously, but that a sad thought kept tugging at his heart. This all meant that he was going to be parted from his beloved little comrade.

He got out of his bed in the middle of that night and went and stood looking down at Sara, who lay asleep with Emily in her arms. Her black hair was spread out on the pillow and Emily's golden-brown hair mingled with it, both of them had lace-ruffled nightgowns, and both had long eyelashes which lay up on their cheeks. Emily looked so like a real child that Captain Crewe felt glad she was there.

"Heigh-ho, little Sara!" he said to himself. "You don't know how much your daddy will miss you."

The next day he took her to Miss Minchin's. He was to sail the next morning. He explained to Miss Minchin that his solicitors had charge of his affairs in England and would give her any advice she wanted, and that they would pay the bills she sent for Sara's expenses. He would write to Sara twice a week, and she was to be given every pleasure she asked for. "She is a sensible little thing, and never wants anything it isn't safe to give her," he said.

Then he went with Sara into her little sitting room and they bade each other goodbye. Sara sat on his knee and held the lapels of his coat in her small hands, and looked long and hard at his face.

"Are you learning me by heart, little Sara?" he said, stroking her hair.

"No," she answered. "I know you by heart. You are inside my heart." And they hugged as if they

would never let each other go.

When the cab drove away from the door, Sara was sitting on the floor of her sitting room, with her hands under her chin and her eyes following it until it had turned the corner of the square. Emily was sitting by her. When Miss Minchin sent her sister, Miss Amelia, to see what the child was doing, she found she could not open the door.

"I have locked it," said a queer, polite little voice from inside. "I want to be quite by myself, please."

Miss Amelia was fat and dumpy, and much in awe of her sister. She was the better-natured person of the two, but she never disobeyed Miss Minchin. She went downstairs again, looking almost alarmed.

"I never saw such a funny, old-fashioned child, sister," she said. "She has locked herself in, and she is not making the least particle of noise."

"It is much better than if she screamed, as some of them do," Miss Minchin answered. "I expected that a child as much spoiled as she is would set the whole house in an uproar. If ever a child was given her own way in everything, she is."

"I've been putting her things away," said Miss Amelia. "I never saw anything like them – sable and ermine on her coats, and beautiful lace on her underclothing. You have seen some of her clothes. What do you think of them?"

"I think they are perfectly ridiculous," replied Miss Minchin, sharply; "but they will look very well at the head of the line when we take the schoolchildren to church on Sunday. She has been provided for as if she were a little princess."

And upstairs in the locked room Sara and Emily sat on the floor and stared at the corner round which the cab had disappeared, while Captain Crewe looked backward, waving and kissing his hand as if he could not bear to stop.

The Caravan Siege

by Alice Massie

The door of the country school was open, and the grey-green hills could peep in, and see the children came from prosperous farms – for the valley was a rich one. The children of farm labourers went chiefly to the school at the other end of the valley. No one could say why the children were divided up like this, but the fact remained that the only badly dressed and hungry-looking child in the south school was Tom Darrington, and he was lame, so that he could not be expected to tramp up to the north end of the valley as his sisters and brothers had done.

Tom was rather a pet in the school. The girls from Croft Farm shared their lunch with him. They were twins, and rode in on ponies, which they put up in stables at the back of the school.

Miss Bolt, the school mistress, with her eyes upon the lovely view, said: "I think you could sing your fairy chorus with great expression on a day like this. Trebles, take one long look at the beautiful hills before you start, and then fix your eyes on me." The voices lifted very prettily:

Fairy folk, fairy folk, down from the mountains,
Pitter pat – fairy feet ringing along.
Pitter pat – pitter pat – like fairy fountains –
Why do you hurry, still singing your song?

"Now, Ida."
Ida blushed and coughed, and began the solo

part awkwardly, but her voice was full, and rich, and rather mournful:

People of earth, we have lost a fair daughter,
Say have you seen her – oh say if you can—

Ida stopped short half-way through her solo; there was a sudden movement through the class. Miss Bolt turned towards the door at the side. Leaning against the doorframe was a slender, graceful girl. She wore shoes but no stockings, and a shabby cotton frock. Her hair stood out like an aureole, and the sun shone through it.

Tommy Darrington said out loud, not knowing that he had spoke: "It's the fairy daughter!"

Miss Bolt said: "What is it, dear?" The girl stepped into the room and came to Miss Bolt's desk. The whole school watched her.

"Oh if you please," said the girl, "I want to come to school. We've just moved into the valley, and Father thought I'd better come."

The whole school gasped. No one had moved into the valley. Was Tommy right – was this a fairy? The Croft Farm girls believed she might be; she was very pretty.

Miss Bolt said: "Ida, take my book and make the class repeat the words of the other verses – they don't know them properly." And she led the newcomer out into the sunshine.

When Miss Bolt came in again every eye was fixed upon her. She smiled, and said: "Tomorrow we shall have a new schoolfellow. Her name is Olga Grey. Now we will go on with the singing."

The next morning, Olga came to school early. She was very pretty, eager to make friends, and bright at lessons. At the lunchtime all the girls hung round her.

Ella Croft said: "Where do you live, Olga?"

Olga replied: "In London, but we're staying here while Daddy's ill."

"She lives—" said Ida, and then stopped.

"Then you're in lodgings?" said Ella. That explained it. One of the farmers had taken them.

"Sort of," said Olga, smiling.

"Sort of!" repeated Ida. Ida, with her lovely voice, had been the unofficial head of the school; she could see at once that this pretty new girl, who could sing nearly as well as she could herself, would be their queen at once.

"She doesn't live anywhere," said Betty Croft. "She's the fairy down from the hills."

Ida sniffed.

When school was over, the Croft girls wanted to ride up the valley with Olga, but she said: "Daddy will come down to meet me, and he can't bear strangers – not till he's stronger if you don't mind."

So the Croft girls watched her running up the track beside the silver birches, looking more than ever like a fairy. When she had passed out of sight, Ida Burman spoke. "I tell you why she won't let you go with her; she's a gypsy; she lives in a caravan!"

Ella and Betty Croft looked at each other, and they laughed. "A gypsy!" said Betty. "With fair hair like that and speaking as she does! You're only jealous, Ida, because she's prettier than you."

"If you had said she was a fairy now—" said Ella.

"I tell you," said Ida, "they came down that track two days ago. My uncle wouldn't let them camp on his land – he didn't want his chickens stolen. Mr Graham let them have his little spinney place."

Ella started her pony. "They're certainly not gypsies," she said.

"They are!" said Ida. "You'll have Olga selling clothes pegs at your door, you see! A girl like that ought not to come to our school."

"Rubbish!" said Betty. But all the same she stopped in the middle of a game of tennis that evening to stare at a pedlar woman who was going to the back door with a basket. Was she possibly a relative of Olga Grey's?

At school Olga was very reticent. Her mother was dead, she and her father lived together and a 'man' of father's cooked for them and looked after them. That startled the school. What sort of man? Rumours floated about of a strange, bent man seen in Mr Graham's spinney, where the van was. Someone said they had seen the van, but was hardly believed, because to get to Mr Graham's spinney you had to go practically across his lawn, and Mr Graham was touchy about his land and trespassers.

On the 23rd of June the school was reading part of Shakespeare's *A Midsummer Night's Dream*, and Tommy Darrington put up his hand.

"Please, teacher," he said, "I seen a fairy dance."

"Have you, Tommy? Where?"

"Back of Mr Graham's house, miss, please. And there was lovely fairy music."

"How delightful! Well, as this is midsummer-eve now, you'd better look out again tonight."

Betty Croft was watching Olga. She saw Olga half turn to Tommy with a startled look in her eye, and a soft flush mounted to her face.

'I believe she is a fairy – really I believe she is,' thought Betty.

Ida Burman put her hand on Betty's rein at close of school, and said, "Doris, and Hetty, and Bill Smith, and myself, and one or two more, we're going up to that caravan tonight – to find out things. We can sneak up between the haycocks and no one will see us. Like to come?"

"No – yes – I don't know," said Betty.

"If they're witches or gypsies we shall smash the windows. They've no right – people like that – to send children to this school."

"Ella and I will come," said Betty, and she put her lips together. She wouldn't let anyone smash Olga's windows. Her brother Jim, the midshipman, was home on leave; she'd make him come. Who cared if Olga's people sold clothes pegs! Olga was a dear.

Up through the hayfield came the conspirators. Betty and Ella and Jim were together. There was the caravan at last, looking ghostly in the evening summer light, and there upon the steps sat Tommy Darrington. Just behind him there was the bent, dark man, and he was playing on a violin. From the tent there came a fairy dressed in something that floated and shimmered.

She glided to the steps of the caravan and began to sway. The violin laughed and sobbed, and the fairy danced and danced.

"It's Olga, and she is a fairy then!" said Betty.

The violinist rose; his back was very crooked. Someone in the hayfield cried: "They're witches. Look – he's humped!" And threw a stone. The dancer ran into the caravan.

Betty, Jim and Ella rose. "Stop that!" cried Jim, in what should have been a splendid naval voice, only it would end in a squeak, because Jim's voice was breaking.

"Mind your own business," cried the stone-thrower. "We're not going to have mad people here, coming to our school!"

Jim and the boy who had thrown grappled with each other; Tommy Darrington stood up and shut the caravan steps and the caravan door, standing against it, outside, waving his crutch.

"Come on!" he cried. "Come on, if you dare!"

No one came; they could hear Jim and the other boy scuffling, pummelling; they could hear unearthly music; and had seen fairy dancing; they were scared; they were angry because they were scared. Under the hedgerow were stones, cleared from the field; some of the children picked them up and threw them at the caravan; many missed, some pattered on the caravan; one hit Tommy.

The evening had clouded over and it was getting dark. A light suddenly appeared in the caravan. The door was opened and a woman stood on the steps. A little cry of amazement went up from the children. It was Miss Bolt, their schoolmistress.

No more stones were thrown. Jim Croft hit his opponent on the nose again and let him go. Miss Bolt just stood there, looking towards them. Nearly everyone ran away. Betty and Ella thought of going to see Miss Bolt and saying they had come to save the caravan, not attack it, but that seemed like boasting. They, too, turned round and went away.

In school next morning most of the children looked worried. If you spent the evening throwing stones at the roof that happened to shelter your schoolmistress, what happened to you? Olga Grey did not appear; Tommy Darrington did not appear.

When Miss Bolt came she said: "Children, your fairy opera performance won't take place. Up to last night I hoped that Sir Gilbert Grey, a world-famous musician, and Olga's father, would help us. By your own actions you have now made that impossible."

A gasp went round the school. Ida Burman murmured: "She should have told us."

Miss Bolt said: "Olga feared to seem superior. She wanted to make friends of you."

Betty Croft said: "Oh, Miss Bolt, isn't she coming any more?"

Miss Bolt shook her head. "No," she said. "The

violinist, who is an old friend of Sir Gilbert's, thinks it better to find a more hospitable valley. They are taking Tommy with them – Sir Gilbert thinks he knows a surgeon who can cure Tommy's leg."

"Teacher, we didn't know."

Miss Bolt rapped the desk. "Know!" she said, "Couldn't you have trusted?" Her eyes rested on Tommy's empty place and softened. "It's better to believe in fairies and take things on trust," she said. "We'll miss the singing lesson. Get out your arithmetic books. Ida Burman, there were three sums wrong in your homework book; you will stay behind and get them right. Billy, close the door – I do not think we wish to see the hills today."

"No, miss," said Billy mournfully. As he closed the door, he thought he heard the creaking of a caravan upon the distant track.

A French Lesson

From *A Little Princess*
by Frances Hodgson Burnett

When Sara entered the schoolroom the next morning everybody looked at her with interested eyes. By that time every pupil had heard a great deal about her. They knew that she was Miss Minchin's show pupil. One or two of them had even caught a glimpse of her French maid, Mariette, who had arrived the evening before. Lavinia had managed to pass Sara's room when the door was open, and had seen Mariette opening a box which had arrived late from some shop.

ALONE IN THE WORLD

"It was full of petticoats with lace frills on them," she whispered to her friend Jessie as she bent over her geography. "I heard Miss Minchin say to Miss Amelia that her clothes were too grand for a child. My mamma says that children should be dressed simply. She has got one of those petticoats on now. I saw it when she sat down."

"She has silk stockings on!" whispered Jessie, bending over her geography also. "And what little feet! I never saw such little feet."

"Oh," sniffed Lavinia, spitefully, "that is the way her slippers are made. My mamma says that even big feet can be made to look small if you have a clever shoemaker. I don't think she is pretty at all. Her eyes are such a queer colour."

"She isn't pretty as other pretty people are," said Jessie,

stealing a glance across the room; "but she makes you want to look at her again. She has very long eyelashes, but her eyes are almost green."

Sara was sitting quietly in her seat. She had been placed near Miss Minchin's desk. She was not abashed at all by the many pairs of eyes watching her. She was interested and looked back quietly at the children who looked at her. She wondered what they were thinking of, and if they liked Miss Minchin, and if they cared for their lessons, and if any of them had a papa at all like her own. She had had a long talk with Emily about her papa that morning.

"He is on the sea now, Emily," she had said. "We

must be very great friends to each other and tell each other things. Emily, you have the nicest eyes I ever saw. But I wish you could speak."

After Mariette had dressed her in her dark-blue schoolroom frock and tied her hair with a dark-blue ribbon, she went to Emily, who sat in a chair of her own, and gave her a book. "You can read that while I am downstairs," she said; and, seeing Mariette looking at her curiously, she spoke to her with a serious little face.

"What I believe about dolls," she said, "is that they can do things they will not let us know about. Perhaps, really, Emily can read and talk and walk, but she will only do it when people are out of the room. You see, if people knew that dolls could do things, they would make them work. So, perhaps, they have promised each other to keep it a secret. If you stay in the room, Emily will just sit there; but if you go out, she will begin to read, or go and look out of the window. Then if she heard either of us coming, she would run back and jump into her chair and pretend she had been there all the time."

"What an odd child!" Mariette said to herself. But she had already begun to like this little girl who had an intelligent face and perfect manners. Sara had a gentle way of saying, 'If you please, Mariette,' which was very charming. Mariette told the head housemaid that she thanked her as if she was thanking a lady. "She has the air of a princess, this little one," she said. Indeed, she was pleased with her new little mistress and liked her place greatly.

After Sara had sat in her seat in the schoolroom for a few minutes, being looked at by the pupils, Miss Minchin rapped in a dignified manner upon her desk.

"Young ladies," she said, "I wish to introduce you to your new companion." All the girls rose in their places, and Sara rose also. "I shall expect you all to be very agreeable to Miss Crewe. As soon as lessons are over you must make each other's acquaintance."

he arrives. Now, return to your desk."

Sara's cheeks felt warm. She went back to her seat and opened the book. She looked at the first page with a grave face. She knew it would be rude to smile, and she was very determined not to be rude. But it was very odd to find herself expected to study a page which told her that '*le pere*' meant 'the father,' and '*la mere*' meant 'the mother.'

'When Monsieur Dufarge comes,' she thought, 'I can make him understand.'

Monsieur Dufarge arrived very shortly afterward. He was a very nice, intelligent, middle-aged Frenchman, and he looked interested when his eyes fell upon Sara.

"Is this a new pupil for me, madame?" he said to Miss Minchin. "I hope that is my good fortune."

"Her papa – Captain Crewe – is very anxious that she should begin the language. But I am afraid she has a childish prejudice against it. She does not seem to wish to learn," said Miss Minchin.

"I am sorry of that, mademoiselle," he said kindly to Sara. "Perhaps, when we begin to study together, I may show you that it is a charming tongue."

Little Sara rose in her seat. She was beginning to feel rather desperate, as if she were in disgrace. She looked up into Monsieur Dufarge's face with her green-grey eyes, and they were quite appealing. She knew that he would understand as soon as she spoke. She began to explain in pretty and fluent French. Madame had not understood. She had not learnt French exactly – not out of books – but her papa had always spoken it to her, and she had read it and written it as she had read and written English. Her papa loved it, because her dear mamma, who had died when she was born, had been French. She would be glad to learn anything monsieur would teach her, but she had tried to explain to madame that she already knew the words in this book – and she held out the little book of phrases.

When she began to speak Miss Minchin started violently and sat staring at her over her glasses, until she had finished. Monsieur Dufarge began to smile, and his smile was one of great pleasure. To hear this pretty voice speaking his language so charmingly made him feel almost as if he were in his native land – which in foggy days in London sometimes seemed worlds away. When she had finished, he took the phrase book from her, with a look almost affectionate. But he spoke to Miss Minchin.

"Ah, madame," he said, "there is not much I can teach her. She has not learnt French; she is French.

Her accent is exquisite."

"You ought to have told me," exclaimed Miss Minchin, much mortified, turning to Sara.

"I – I tried," said Sara. "I – I suppose I did not begin right."

Miss Minchin knew she had tried, and that it had not been her fault that she was not allowed to explain. And when she saw that the pupils had been listening and that Lavinia and Jessie were giggling behind their French grammars, she felt infuriated.

"Silence, young ladies!" she said severely, rapping upon the desk. "Silence at once!"

And she began from that minute to feel rather a grudge against her show pupil.

Two Visits and What Came of Them

From *Heidi*
by Johanna Spyri

*Aged five, the orphan Heidi is taken by her cousin to live with
her grandfather, a herdsman who lives up the side of a mountain
in the Swiss Alps. Grandfather and Heidi live contentedly until the
outside world intrudes and threatens to separate them.*

Quickly the winter passed, and still more quickly
the bright glad summer, and now another
winter was drawing to its close. Heidi was as light-
hearted as the birds, and looked forward with more

delight each day to the coming spring.

Heidi was now in her eighth year; she had learnt all kinds of useful things from her grandfather; she knew how to look after the goats as well as any one, and Little Swan and Bear would follow her like two faithful dogs, giving bleats of pleasure when they heard her voice. Twice during the course of this last winter Peter had brought up a message from the schoolmaster at Dorfli, who sent word to Alm-Uncle that he ought to send Heidi to school. Uncle had sent word back each time that the schoolmaster would find him at home if he had anything he wished to say to him, but that he did not intend to send Heidi to school.

When the March sun had melted the snow on the mountain side and the snowdrops were peeping out all over the valley, and the fir trees had shaken off their burden of snow and were again waving their branches in the air, Heidi ran backwards and forwards with delight first to the goat-shed then to the fir-trees, and then to the hut-door, in order to let her grandfather know how much larger a piece of green there was under thc trees, and then would run off to look again, for she could hardly wait till everything was green and the full summer had clothed the mountain with grass and flowers.

As Heidi was running about one sunny March morning, and had just jumped over the water-trough for the tenth time, she nearly fell backwards into it with fright, for there in front of her, looking gravely at her, stood an old gentleman dressed in black. When he saw how startled she was, he said in a kind voice, "Don't be afraid of me. You must be Heidi; where is your grandfather?"

"He is sitting by the table, making wooden spoons," Heidi told him, as she opened the door.

He was the old village pastor from Dorfli who had been a neighbour of Uncle's when he lived down there. He stepped inside the hut, and going up to the old man, who was bending over his work,

said, "Good morning, neighbour."

The grandfather looked up in surprise, and then rising said, "Good morning" in return. He pushed a chair towards the visitor as he continued, "If you do not mind a wooden seat there is one for you."

The pastor sat down. "I have come today to talk over something with you," he said. "I think you know already what it is that has brought me here," and as he spoke he looked towards the child who was standing at the door, gazing with interest and surprise at the stranger.

"Heidi, go to the goats," said her grandfather. Take them some salt and stay there till I come." Heidi vanished on the spot.

"The child ought to have been at school a year ago, and most certainly this last winter," said the pastor. "The schoolmaster sent you word about it. What are you thinking of doing with the child?"

"I am thinking of not sending her to school," was the answer.

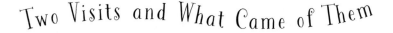

The visitor looked across at the old man, who was sitting with his arms crossed and a determined expression about his whole person. "How are you going to let her grow up then?" he asked.

"I am going to let her grow up and be happy among the goats and birds; with them she is safe, and will learn nothing evil."

"But the child is not a goat, she is a human being. She ought not to grow up in ignorance, and it is time she began her lessons. I have come now that you may have leisure to think over it, and to arrange about it during the summer. This is the last winter that she must be allowed to run wild; next winter she must come regularly to school every day."

"She will do no such thing," said the old man.

"Do you mean that by no persuasion can you be brought to see reason?" said the pastor, growing somewhat angry. "You have been about the world, and must have learnt much, and I should have given you credit for more sense, neighbour."

"Indeed," replied the old man, and there was a tone in his voice that betrayed a growing irritation on his part too, "and does the worthy pastor really mean that he would wish me next winter to send a child like that some miles down the mountain through storms, and let her return at night, when even we would run a risk of being buried in the snow? And perhaps he may not have forgotten the child's mother, Adelaide? She was a sleep-walker, and had fits. Might not the child be attacked in the same way if obliged to over-exert herself? I will go before all the courts of justice in the country, and then we shall see who will force me to do it!"

"You are quite right, neighbour," said the pastor in a friendly tone of voice. "It would have been impossible to send the child to school from here. But I perceive that the child is dear to you; for her sake come down into Dorfli and live again among your fellowmen. If anything were to happen to you up here who would there be to help you? I cannot think but what you must be half frozen to death in this hut in the winter, and I do not know how the child lives through it!"

"The child has young blood in her veins and a good roof over her head, and let me further tell the pastor, that I know where wood is to be found, and when is the proper time to fetch it; the pastor can go and look inside my woodshed; the fire is never out in my hut the whole winter through. As to going to live below that is far from my thoughts; the people despise me and I them; it is therefore best for all of us that we live apart."

"No, no, it is not best for you," said the pastor in an earnest voice. "As to the people down there looking on you with dislike, it is not as bad as you think. Seek to make your peace with God, pray for forgiveness where you need it, and then come and see how differently people will look upon you, and how happy you may yet be."

The pastor had risen and stood holding out his

hand to the old man as he added with earnestness, "I will wager, neighbour, that next winter you will be down among us again, and we shall be good neighbours as of old. Give me your hand and promise me that you will come and live with us again and become reconciled to God and man."

Alm-Uncle gave the pastor his hand and answered him firmly, "You mean well, but I say now what I shall continue to say, that I will not send the child to school nor come and live among you."

"Then God help you!" said the pastor, and he left the hut and went down the mountain.

Alm-Uncle was out of humour. When Heidi said as usual that afternoon, "Can we go down to grandmother now?" he answered, "Not today." The following morning when Heidi again asked the same question, he replied, "We will see."

But before the dinner bowls had been cleared away another visitor arrived, and this time it was Cousin Dete. She had a fine feathered hat on her head, and a long skirt to her dress which swept the floor, and on the floor of a goatherd's hut there are all sorts of things that do not belong to a dress.

The grandfather looked her up and down without uttering a word. But Dete was prepared with an exceedingly amiable speech and began at once to praise the looks of the child. She was looking so well she should hardly have known her again, and it was evident that she had been well-cared for with her grandfather; but she had never lost sight of the idea of taking the child back again, for she well understood that the little one must be much in his way. Day and night she had thought over the means of placing the child somewhere, and she had just heard of something that would be a

Alm-Uncle's way or he may hurt you!"

The old man took no notice of anybody as he strode through the village on his way to the valley below, where he sold his cheeses and bought what bread and meat he wanted for himself. After he had passed the villagers each had something to say about him; how much wilder he looked than usual, how now he would not even respond to anybody's greeting, while they all agreed that it was a great mercy the child had got away from him, and had they not all noticed how the child had hurried along as if afraid that her grandfather might be following to take her back?

Only the blind grandmother would have nothing to say against him, and told those who came to her to bring her work, or take away what she had spun, how kind he had been with the child, how good to her and her daughter, and how many afternoons he had spent mending the house which, but for his help, would certainly by this time have fallen down

over their heads. All this was repeated down in
Dorfli; but most people who heard it said that
grandmother was too old to understand, and very
likely had not heard rightly what was said; as she
was blind she was probably also deaf.

Alm-Uncle went no more now to the
grandmother's house, and it was well that he had
made it so safe, for it was not touched again for a
long time. The days were sad again
now for the old blind woman,
and not one passed but what she
would murmur complainingly,
"Alas! all our happiness and
pleasure have gone with the child,
and now the days are so long and
dreary! Pray God, I see Heidi
again once more before I die!"

NEW FRIENDS

Ginger

From *Black Beauty*
by Anna Sewell

*Black Beauty is written as the autobiography of a young horse.
At the beginning of this extract he has just met Ginger, a chestnut
filly who was to become a lifelong companion, and all is well
in his life as he has a good and kind owner.*

One day when Ginger and I were standing alone
in the shade, she wanted to know all about my
bringing up and breaking in, and I told her.

"Well," said she, "if I had had your bringing up I
might have had as good a temper as you, but now
I don't believe I ever shall."

"Why not?" I said.

"Because it has been all so different with me," she replied. "I never had any one, horse or man, that was kind to me, or that I cared to please. I was taken from my mother as soon as I was weaned, and put with lots of other young colts; none of them cared for me, and I cared for none of them. There was no kind master to look after me, and bring me nice things to eat. The man that had the care of us never gave me a kind word. I do not mean that he ill-used me, but he did not care for us one bit further than to see that we had plenty to eat, and shelter.

"A footpath ran through our field, and very often the boys passing through would fling stones to make us gallop. One fine young colt was badly cut in the face. We settled it in our minds that boys were our enemies.

"But when it came to breaking in, that was a bad time for me; several men came to catch me, and when at last they closed me in at one corner of the

field, one caught me by the forelock, another caught me by the nose and held it so tight I could hardly draw my breath; then another took my under jaw in his hard hand and wrenched my mouth open, and so by force they got on the halter and the bar into my mouth; then one dragged me along by the halter, another flogging behind, and this was the first experience I had of men's kindness; it was all force. They did not give me a chance to know what they wanted. I had a great deal of spirit, and was very wild, and gave them, I dare say, plenty of trouble, but then it was dreadful to be shut up in a stall day after day instead of having my liberty, and I fretted and pined and wanted to get loose.

"There was one – the old master, Mr Ryder – who, I think, could soon have brought me round, and could have done anything with me; but he had given up all the hard part of the trade to his son and to another experienced man, and he only came at times to oversee.

"His son was a strong, tall, bold man; they called him Samson, and he used to boast that he had never found a horse that could throw him. There was no gentleness in him, but only hardness, a hard voice, a hard eye, a hard hand; and I felt from the first that what he wanted was to wear all the spirit out of me, and just make me into a quiet, humble, obedient piece of horseflesh. 'Horseflesh!' Yes, that is all that he thought about," and Ginger stamped her foot as if the thought of him made her angry.

Then she went on: "If I did not do exactly what he wanted he would get put out, and make me run round with that long rein in the training field till he had tired me out.

"One day he had worked me hard in every way he could, and when I lay down I was tired, and miserable, and angry; it all seemed so hard. The next morning he came for me early, and ran me round again for a long time. I had scarcely had an hour's rest, when he came again for me with a

saddle and bridle and a new kind of bit. I could never quite tell how it came about; he had only just mounted me on the training ground, when something I did put him out of temper, and he chucked me hard with the rein. The new bit was very painful, and I reared up suddenly, which angered him still more, and he began to flog me.

"I felt my whole spirit set against him. I began to kick, and plunge, and rear as I had never done before; for a long time he stuck to the saddle and punished me cruelly with his whip and spurs, but I cared for nothing he could do if only I could get him off. At last after a terrible struggle I threw him off backward. I heard him fall heavily on the turf, and without looking behind me, I galloped off to the other end of the field; there I turned round and saw my persecutor slowly rising from the ground and going into the stable.

"I stood under an oak tree and watched, but no one came to catch me. The time went on, and the

sun was very hot; the flies swarmed round me and settled on my bleeding flanks where the spurs had dug in. I felt hungry, for I had not eaten since the early morning, but there was not enough grass in that meadow for a goose to live on.

"I wanted to lie down and rest, but with the saddle strapped on there was no comfort. The afternoon wore on. I saw the other colts led in, and I knew they were having a good feed.

"At last, just as the sun went down, I saw the old master come out with a sieve in his hand. He was a very fine old gentleman with quite white hair, but his voice was what I should know him by among a thousand. It was not high, nor yet low, but full, and clear, and kind, and when he gave orders it was so steady and decided that every one knew, both horses and men, that he expected to be obeyed.

"He came quietly along, shaking the oats that he had in the sieve, and speaking cheerfully and gently to me: 'Come along, lassie; come along.' I stood still and let him come up; he held the oats to me, and I began to eat without fear. He stood by, patting and stroking me while I was eating, and seeing the clots of blood on my side he seemed very vexed. 'Poor lassie! it was a bad business;' then he quietly took the rein and led me to the stable. At the door stood Samson. I laid my ears back and snapped at him. 'Stand back,' said the master, 'and keep out of her way; you've done a bad day's work for this filly.' He growled something about a vicious brute. 'Hark ye,' said the father, 'a bad-tempered man will never make a good-tempered horse. You've not learnt your trade yet, Samson.'

"Then he led me into my box, took off the saddle and bridle with his own hands, and tied me up; then he called for a pail of warm water and a sponge, took off his coat, and while the stable-man held the pail, he sponged my sides so tenderly that I was sure he knew how sore and bruised they were. 'Whoa! my pretty one,' he said, 'stand still, stand still.' His very voice did me good, and the bathing was very comfortable. The skin was so broken at the corners of my mouth that I could not eat the hay. He looked closely at it, shook his head, and told the man to fetch a good bran mash and put some meal into it. How good that mash was! So soft and healing to my mouth. He stood by all the time I was eating, stroking me and talking to the man. 'If a high-mettled creature like this,' said he, 'can't be broken by fair means, she will never be good for anything.'

"After that he often came to see me, and when my mouth was healed the other breaker, Job, went on training me; he was steady and thoughtful, and I soon learnt what he wanted." And so Ginger finished telling me about her bad start in life.

The Key to the Garden

From *The Secret Garden*
by Frances Hodgson Burnett

*Mary Lennox is the spoiled orphan daughter of a British official in
India who is brought back to Misselthwaite Manor in Yorkshire,
England, to live with her uncle, a disabled and reclusive man.*

When Mary opened her eyes she sat upright in
bed immediately, and called to Martha.
"Look at the moor! Look at the moor!"
The rainstorm had ended and the grey mist and
clouds had been swept away in the night by the
wind. The wind had ceased and a brilliant, deep
blue sky arched high over the moorland. Never had

Mary dreamed of a sky so blue. In India skies were
hot and blazing; this was a deep cool blue which
almost seemed to sparkle like the waters of some
lovely bottomless lake. Here and there, high in the
arched blueness floated small clouds of snow-white
fleece. The far-reaching world of the moor itself
looked softly blue instead of gloomy purple-black
or dreary grey.

"Aye," said Martha with a cheerful grin. "Th' storm's over for a bit. It does like this at this time o' th' year. It goes off in a night like it was pretendin' it had never been here an' never meant to come again. That's because th' springtime's on its way. It's a long way off yet, but it's comin'."

"I thought perhaps it always rained or looked dark in England," Mary said.

"Eh! no!" said Martha, sitting up on her heels among her black lead brushes. "Nowt o' th' soart!"

"What does that mean?" asked Mary seriously. In India, natives spoke different dialects which only a few people understood, so she was not surprised when Martha used words she did not know.

"There now," Martha said. "I've talked broad Yorkshire again like Mrs Medlock said I mustn't. 'Nowt o' th' soart' means 'nothin'-of-the-sort'," slowly and carefully, "but it takes so long to say it. Yorkshire's th' sunniest place on earth when it is sunny. I told thee tha'd like th' moor after a bit. Just you wait till you see th' gold-coloured gorse blossoms an' th' blossoms o' th' broom, an' th' heather flowerin', all purple bells, an' hundreds o' butterflies flutterin' an' bees hummin' an' skylarks soarin' up an' singin'. You'll want to get out on it as sunrise an' live out on it all day like Dickon does."

"Could I ever get there?" asked Mary wistfully, looking through her window at the far-off blue.

"I don't know," said Martha. "Tha's never used tha' legs since tha' was born, it seems. Tha' couldn't walk five mile. It's five mile to our cottage."

"I should like to see your cottage."

Martha stared at her a moment curiously before she took up her polishing brush again. She was thinking that the small plain face did not look quite as sour as it had done the first morning she saw it.

"I'll ask my mother about it," she said. "She's one o' them that nearly always sees a way to do things. It's my day out today an' I'm goin' home. Eh! I am glad. Mrs Medlock thinks a lot o' mother. Perhaps she could talk to her."

"I like your mother," said Mary.

"I should think tha' did," agreed Martha, polishing away.

"I've never seen her," said Mary.

"No, tha' hasn't," replied Martha.

She sat up on her heels again and rubbed the end of her nose with the back of her hand as if puzzled for a moment, but she ended quite positively.

"Well, she's that sensible an' hard workin' an' goodnatured an' clean that no one could help likin' her whether they'd seen her or not. When I'm goin' home to her on my day out I just jump for joy when I'm crossin' the moor."

"I like Dickon," added Mary, "And I've never seen him."

"Well," said Martha stoutly, "I've told thee that th' birds likes him an' th' rabbits an' wild sheep an' ponies, an' th' foxes. I wonder," staring at her reflectively, "what Dickon would think of thee?"

"He wouldn't like me," said Mary in her stiff, cold little way. "No one does."

Martha looked reflective again.

"How does tha' like thysel'?" she inquired, really quite as if she were curious to know.

Mary hesitated and thought it over. "Not at all, really," she answered. "But I never thought of that before."

Martha grinned a little as if at some homely recollection. "Mother said that to me once," she said. "She was at her wash-tub an' I was in a bad temper an' talkin' ill of folk, an' she says: 'Tha' young vixen, tha'! There tha' stands sayin' tha' doesn't like this one an' tha' doesn't like that one. How does tha' like thysel'?' It made me laugh an' it brought me to my senses in a minute."

She went away in high spirits as soon as she had given Mary her breakfast. She was going to walk five miles across the moor to the cottage, and she was going to help her mother with the washing and do the week's baking and enjoy herself thoroughly.

Mary went out into the garden as quickly as possible, and the first thing she did was to run round the fountain flower garden ten times. When she had finished she felt better. She went into the first kitchen-garden and found Ben Weatherstaff there with two other gardeners. The change in the weather seemed to have done him good. He spoke to her of his own accord. "Spring's comin'," he said.

"Cannot tha' smell it?"

Mary sniffed and thought she could. "I smell something nice and fresh and damp," she said.

"That's th' good rich earth," he answered, digging away. "It's glad when plantin' time comes. It's dull in th' winter when it's got nowt to do. In th' flower gardens out there you'll see bits o' green spikes stickin' out o' th' earth after a bit."

"What will they be?" asked Mary.

"Crocuses, snowdrops an' daffydowndillys. Has tha' never seen them?"

"No. Everything is hot, and wet, and green after the rains in India," said Mary. "And I think things grow up in a night."

"These won't grow up in a night," said Weatherstaff. "Tha'll have to wait for 'em. They'll poke up a bit higher here, an' push out a spike more there, an' uncurl a leaf this day an' another that. You watch 'em."

"I am going to," answered Mary.

Very soon she heard the soft rustling flight of wings again and she knew at once that the robin had come again. He was very pert and lively, and hopped briskly about so close to her feet that she asked Ben Weatherstaff, "Do you think he remembers me?"

"Remembers thee!" said Ben Weatherstaff indignantly. "He knows every cabbage stump in th' gardens, let alone th' people. He's never seen a little girl here before, an' he's bent on findin' out all about thee."

"Are things stirring down below in the dark in that garden where he lives?" Mary inquired.

"What garden?" grunted Ben Weatherstaff, becoming surly again.

"The one where the old rose-trees are." She could not help asking, she wanted so much to know. "Are all the flowers dead, or do some of them come again in the summer? Are there any roses?"

"Ask him," said Ben Weatherstaff, hunching his

shoulders toward the robin. "He's the only one as knows. No one else has seen inside it for ten year.'"

Ten years was a long time, Mary thought. She had been born ten years ago.

She walked away, slowly thinking. She had begun to like the garden just as she had begun to like the robin and Dickon and Martha's mother. She was beginning to like Martha, too. That seemed a good many people to like – when you were not used to liking. She thought of the robin as one of the people. She went to her walk outside the long, ivy-covered wall over which she could see the tree-tops; and the second time she walked up and down the most interesting and exciting thing happened to her.

She heard a chirp and a twitter, and when she looked at the bare flower-bed at her left side there he was hopping about and pretending to peck things out of the earth to persuade her that he had not followed her. But she knew he had followed her and the surprise so filled her with delight that she almost trembled a little.

"You do remember me!" she cried out. "You do! You are prettier than anything else in the world!"

She talked, and coaxed and he hopped, and flirted his tail and twittered. It was as if he were talking. He allowed her to draw closer and closer to him, and bend down and talk and try to make something like robin sounds.

To think that he should actually let her come as near to him as that! He knew nothing in the world would make her put out her hand toward him or startle him in the tiniest way. He knew it because he was a real person – only nicer than any other person in the world. The flower-bed was not quite bare. It was bare of flowers, but there were tall shrubs and low ones which grew together at the back of the bed, and as the robin hopped about under them she saw him hop over a small pile of freshly turned up earth. He stopped on it to look for a worm. The earth had been turned up because a dog had been

trying to dig up a mole and he
had scratched quite a
deep hole.

Mary looked at it,
not really knowing
why the hole was
there, and as she looked she saw something almost
buried in the newly-turned soil. It was something
like a ring of rusty iron or brass and when the robin
flew up into a tree nearby she put out her hand and
picked the ring up. It was more than a ring,
however; it was an old key that looked as if it had
been buried a long time.

Mistress Mary stood up and looked at it with an
almost frightened face as it hung from her finger.
"Perhaps it has been buried for ten years," she said
in a whisper. "Perhaps it is the key to the garden!"

The Riverbank

From *The Wind in the Willows*
by Kenneth Grahame

The Mole had been working very hard all the morning, spring-cleaning his little home. First with brooms, then with dusters; then on ladders and steps and chairs, with a brush and a pail of whitewash; till he had dust in his throat and eyes, and splashes of whitewash all over his black fur, and an aching back and weary arms. Spring was moving in the air above and in the earth below and around him, penetrating even his dark and lowly little house with its spirit of divine discontent and longing.

It was small wonder, then, that he suddenly flung down his brush on the floor, said "Bother!" and "Oh blow!" and also "Hang spring-cleaning!" and bolted out of the house without even waiting to put on his coat. Something up above was calling him imperiously, and he made for the steep little tunnel, which answered in his case to the gravelled carriage-drive owned by animals whose residences are nearer to the sun and air. So he worked busily with his little paws and muttering to himself, "Up we go! Up we go!" till at last, *pop!* His snout came out into the sunlight, and he found himself rolling in the warm grass of a great meadow.

"This is fine!" he said to himself. "This is better than whitewashing!" The sunshine struck hot on his fur, soft breezes caressed his heated brow, and the carol of happy birds fell on his dulled hearing almost like a shout. Jumping off all his legs at once, in the joy of living and the delight of spring without its cleaning, he pursued his way across the meadow till he reached the hedge on the further side.

Hither and thither through the meadows he rambled busily, along the hedgerows, across the copses, finding everywhere birds building, flowers budding, leaves thrusting – everything happy. And instead of having an uneasy conscience whispering 'whitewash!' he somehow could only feel how jolly it was to be the only idle dog among all these busy citizens. After all, the best part of a holiday is perhaps not so much to be resting yourself, as to see all the other fellows busy working.

He thought his happiness was complete when, as he meandered aimlessly along, suddenly he stood by the edge of a full-fed river. Never in his life had he seen a river before – this sleek, sinuous, full-bodied animal, chasing and chuckling, gripping things with a gurgle and leaving them with a laugh. All was a-shake and a-shiver – glints and gleams and sparkles, rustle and swirl, chatter and bubble. The Mole was bewitched, entranced, fascinated. By

the side of the river he trotted, and when tired at
last, he sat on the bank, while the river still
chattered on to him, a babbling procession of the
best stories in the world, sent from the heart of the
earth to be told at last to the insatiable sea.

As he sat on the grass and looked across the river,
a dark hole in the bank opposite, just above the
water's edge, caught his eye, and dreamily he fell to
considering what a nice snug dwelling-place it
would make for an animal with few wants and fond
of a riverside residence, above flood level and
remote from noise and dust. As he gazed,
something bright and small seemed to twinkle
down in the heart of it, vanished, then twinkled
once more like a tiny star. Then, as he looked, it
winked at him, and so declared itself to be an eye,
and a small face began gradually to grow up round
it, like a frame round a picture.

A brown little face, with whiskers.

A grave round face, with the twinkle in its eye

that had first caught his notice.
Neat ears and thick silky hair.
It was the Water Rat!
Then the two animals stood and
regarded each other cautiously.
"Hullo, Mole!" said the Water Rat.
"Hullo, Rat!" said the Mole.
"Would you like to come over?"
enquired the Rat presently.
"Oh, its all very well to talk," said
the Mole, rather pettishly, he being
new to riverside life and its ways.
The Rat said nothing, but stooped
and unfastened a rope and hauled
on it; then lightly stepped into
a little boat, which the Mole
had not observed. It was just
the size for two animals; and the
Mole's whole heart went out to it
at once.

103

The Rat sculled smartly across and made fast. Then he held up his forepaw as the Mole stepped gingerly down. "Lean on that!" he said. "Now then, step lively!" and the Mole to his surprise found himself seated in the stern of a real boat.

"This has been a wonderful day!" said he, as the Rat shoved off and took to the sculls again. "I've never been in a boat before in all my life."

"What?" cried the Rat, open-mouthed: "Never been in a – you never – well I – what have you been doing, then?"

"Is it so nice as all that?" asked the Mole shyly.

"Nice? It's the only thing," said the Water Rat solemnly. "Believe me there is nothing half so much worth doing as simply messing about in boats. Simply messing..." he went on dreamily, "messing... about... in... boats... messing..."

"Look ahead, Rat!" cried the Mole suddenly.

It was too late. The boat struck the bank full tilt. The joyous oarsman lay on his back at the bottom of the boat, his heels in the air.

"—about in boats or with boats," the Rat went on composedly, picking himself up with a pleasant laugh. "In or out of 'em, it doesn't matter. Whether you get away, or whether you don't; whether you arrive at your destination or whether you reach somewhere else, or whether you never get anywhere at all, you're always busy, and you never do anything in particular; and when you've done it there's always something else to do.

"Look here! If you've really nothing else on hand this morning, supposing we drop down the river together, and have a day of it?"

The Mole waggled his toes from sheer happiness, spread his chest with a sigh of full contentment, and leant back into the soft cushions. "What a day I'm having!" he said. "Let us start at once!"

"Hold hard a minute, then!" said the Rat. He looped the painter through a ring in his landing-stage, climbed up into his hole above, and after a

short interval reappeared staggering under a fat, wicker luncheon-basket.

"Shove that under your feet," he observed to the Mole, as he passed it down into the boat. Then he untied the painter and took the sculls again.

"What's inside it?" asked the Mole, wriggling with curiosity.

"There's cold chicken inside it," replied the Rat briefly; "coldtonguecoldhamcoldbeefpickled gherkinssaladfrenchrollscresssandwichespottedmeat gingerbeerlemonadesodawater—"

"Oh stop, stop," cried the Mole in ecstacies: "This is too much!"

"Do you really think so?" enquired the Rat seriously. "It's only what I always take on these little excursions."

The Mole never heard a word he was saying. Absorbed in the new life he was entering upon, intoxicated with the sparkle, the ripple, the scents and the sounds and the sunlight, he trailed a paw in

106

the water and dreamed long waking dreams. The Water Rat, like the good little fellow he was, sculled steadily on and forebore to disturb him.

"I like your clothes awfully, old chap," he remarked after some half an hour or so had passed. "I'm going to get a black velvet smoking-suit myself some day, as soon as I can afford it."

"I beg your pardon," said the Mole, pulling himself together with an effort. "You must think me very rude, but all this is so new to me. So... this... is... a... river!"

"The River," corrected the Rat.

"And you live by the river? What a jolly life!"

"By it and with it and on it and in it," said the Rat. "It's brother and sister to me, and aunts, and company, and food and drink, and (naturally) washing. It's my world, and I don't want any other."

"But isn't it a bit dull at times?" the Mole ventured to ask. "Just you and the river, and no one else to pass a word with?"

tree-roots gleamed below the surface of the water, while ahead of them the foamy tumble of a weir, arm-in-arm with a restless dripping mill-wheel, that held up in its turn a grey-gabled mill-house, filled the air with a soothing murmur of sound. It was so very beautiful that the Mole could only hold up both forepaws and gasp, "Oh my! Oh my! Oh my!"

The Rat brought the boat alongside the bank, made her fast, helped the still awkward Mole safely ashore, and swung out the luncheon-basket. The Mole begged to be allowed to unpack it, and the Rat was very pleased to sprawl at full length on the grass and rest, while his excited friend shook out the table cloth, took out all the packets one by one and arranged their contents, still gasping, "Oh my! Oh my!" at each fresh revelation.

When all was ready, the Rat said, "Now, pitch in, old fellow!" and the Mole was indeed very glad to obey, for he had started his spring-cleaning at a very early hour that morning, as people will do, and

had not paused for bite or sup.

"What are you looking at?" said the Rat presently, when the edge of their hunger was somewhat dulled, and the Mole's eyes were able to wander off the table cloth a little.

"I am looking," said the Mole, "at a streak of bubbles that I see travelling along the surface of the water. That is a thing that strikes me as funny."

"Bubbles? Oho!" said the Rat, and chirruped cheerily in an inviting sort of way.

A broad glistening muzzle showed itself above the edge of the bank, and the Otter hauled himself out and shook the water from his coat.

"Greedy beggars!" he observed, making for the provender. "Why didn't you invite me, Ratty?"

"This was an impromptu affair," explained the Rat. "By the way – my friend Mr Mole."

"Proud, I'm sure," said the Otter, and the two animals were friends forthwith.

"Such a rumpus everywhere!" continued the

Otter. "All the world seems out on the river today. I came up this backwater to try and get a moment's peace, and stumble upon you fellows! At least – I beg pardon – I don't exactly mean that, you know."

There was a rustle behind them, proceeding from a hedge wherein last year's leaves still clung thick, and a stripy head, with high shoulders behind it, peered forth on them.

"Come on, old Badger!" shouted the Rat.

The Badger trotted forward a pace or two; then grunted, "H'm! Company," and turned his back and disappeared from view.

"That's just the sort of fellow he is!" observed the disappointed Rat. "Now we shan't see any more of him today. Well, tell us, who's out on the river?"

"Toad's out, for one," replied the Otter. "In his new wager-boat – new togs, new everything!" The two animals looked at each other and laughed.

"Once, it was nothing but sailing," said the Rat, "Then he tired of that and took to punting.

Nothing would please him but to punt all day and every day, and a nice mess he made of it. Last year it was house-boating, and we all had to go and stay with him in his house-boat, and pretend we liked it. He was going to spend the rest of his life in a house-boat. It's all the same, whatever he takes up; he gets tired of it, and starts on something fresh."

"Such a good fellow, too," remarked the Otter reflectively. "But no stability – especially in a boat!"

From where they sat they could get a glimpse of the main stream across the island that separated them; and just then a wager-boat flashed into view, the rower – a short, stout figure – splashing badly and rolling a good deal, but working his hardest.

"He'll be out of the boat in a minute if he rolls like that," said the Rat.

"Of course he will," chuckled the Otter. "Did I ever tell you that good story about Toad and the lock-keeper? It happened this way. Toad..."

An errant May-fly swerved unsteadily athwart

the current in the intoxicated fashion affected by
young bloods of May-flies seeing life. A swirl of
water and a '*cloop!*' and the May-fly was visible
no more.

Neither was the Otter.

The Mole looked down. The voice was still in
his ears, but the turf whereon he had sprawled was
vacant. Not an Otter to be seen. But again there
was a streak of bubbles on the surface of the river.

"Well, well," said the Rat, "I suppose we ought to
be moving. I wonder which of us had better pack
the luncheon-basket?" He did not speak as if he was
frightfully eager for the treat.

"Oh, please let me," said the Mole. So, of course,
the Rat let him.

Packing the basket was not quite such pleasant
work as unpacking the basket. But the Mole was
bent on enjoying everything, and although just
when he had got the basket packed and strapped up
tightly he saw a plate staring up at him from the

– the Mole could feel him laughing, right down his arm and through his paw.

The Rat got hold of a scull and shoved it under the Mole's arm; then he did the same by the other side of him and, swimming behind, propelled the helpless animal to shore, hauled him out, and set him on the bank, a squashy, pulpy lump of misery.

When the Rat had rubbed him down a bit, and wrung some of the wet out of him, he said, "Now, then, old fellow! Trot up and down the towing-path as hard as you can, till you're warm and dry again, while I dive for the luncheon-basket."

So the dismal Mole, wet without and ashamed within, trotted about till he was fairly dry, while the Rat plunged into the water again, recovered the boat, righted her, fetched his floating property to shore by degrees, and finally dived successfully for the luncheon-basket and struggled to land with it.

When all was ready for a start once more, the Mole, limp and dejected, took his seat in the stern of the boat; and as they set off, he said in a low voice, "Ratty, my generous friend! I am very sorry for my foolish and ungrateful conduct. My heart fails me when I think how I might have lost that beautiful basket. Indeed, I have been a complete ass, and I know it. Will you overlook it this once and forgive me, and let things go on as before?"

"That's all right, bless you!" responded the Rat cheerily. "What's a little wet to a water rat? I'm more in the water than out of it most days. Don't

you think any more about it. Look here! I really think you had better come and stop with me for a little time. It's very plain and rough, you know – not like Toad's house at all – but you haven't seen that yet. Still, I can make you comfortable. And I'll teach you to row, and to swim, and you'll soon be as handy on the water as any of us."

The Mole was so touched by his kind manner that he could find no voice to answer him, and he had to brush away a tear with the back of his paw. But the Rat kindly looked in another direction, and presently the Mole's spirits revived again.

When they got home, the Rat made a bright fire in the parlour, planted the Mole in an armchair in front of it (having fetched down a dressing-gown and slippers for him), and told him river stories till supper-time. Very thrilling stories they were, too, to an earth-dwelling animal like Mole. Stories about weirs, and sudden floods, and leaping pike; about herons, and how particular they were whom they

spoke to; and about adventures down drains, and
night-fishings with Otter, or excursions far afield
with Badger. Supper was a cheerful meal; but
shortly afterwards a terribly sleepy Mole had to be
escorted upstairs by his considerate host, to the best
bedroom, where he soon laid his head on his pillow
in great peace and contentment, knowing that his
new-found friend the River was lapping the sill of
his window.

This day was only the first of many for the
emancipated Mole, each of them longer and full of
interest as the ripening summer moved onward. He
learnt to swim and to row, and entered into the joy
of running water; and with his ear to the reed-stems
he caught, at intervals, something of what the wind
went whispering so constantly among them.

The Journey Begins

From *The Wonderful Wizard of Oz*
by L Frank Baum

*Dorothy is carried in her house by a cyclone from Kansas to the land
of Oz. When her house kills the Wicked Witch, Dorothy is hailed as a
friend by the Munchkins. She is told that to find her way home she must
ask for the help of the Wizard of Oz, who lives in the City of Emeralds
at the end of the yellow brick road.*

When Dorothy was left alone she began to feel
hungry. So she went to the cupboard and cut
herself some bread, which she spread with butter.
She gave some to Toto, and taking a pail from the
shelf she carried it down to the little brook and

filled it with clear, sparkling water. Toto ran over to the trees and began to bark at the birds sitting there. Dorothy went to get him, and saw such delicious fruit hanging from the branches that she gathered some of it, finding it just what she wanted to help out her breakfast. Then she went back to the house, helped herself and Toto to a good drink of the cool water, and set about making ready for the journey to the City of Emeralds.

Dorothy had only one other dress, but that happened to be clean and was hanging on a peg beside her bed. It was gingham, with checks of white and blue. The girl washed herself, dressed in the clean gingham, and tied her pink sunbonnet on her head. She took a little basket and filled it with bread from the cupboard, laying a white cloth over the top. Then she looked down at her feet and noticed how worn her shoes were.

"They surely will never do for a long journey, Toto," she said. And Toto looked up into her face

with his little black eyes and wagged his tail to show he knew what she meant.

At that moment Dorothy saw lying on the table the silver shoes that had belonged to the Witch of the East. "I wonder if they will fit me," she said to Toto. "They would be just the thing to take a long walk in, for they could not wear out."

She took off her old leather shoes and tried on the silver ones, which fitted her as well as if they had been made for her.

Finally she picked up her basket. "Come along, Toto," she said. "We will go to the Emerald City and ask the Great Oz how to get back to Kansas."

She closed the door, locked it, and put the key carefully in the pocket of her dress. And so, with Toto trotting along soberly behind her, she started on her journey.

There were several roads nearby, but it did not take her long to find the

one paved with yellow bricks. Within a short time
she was walking briskly toward the Emerald City,
her silver shoes tinkling merrily on the hard, yellow
road. The sun shone bright and the birds sang
sweetly, and Dorothy did not feel nearly so
bad as you might think a little girl would
who had been suddenly whisked away from
her own country and set down in the midst
of a strange land.

She was surprised, as she walked along, to
see how pretty the country was about her.
There were neat fences at the sides of the
road, painted a dainty blue, and beyond
them were fields of grain and
vegetables in abundance. Evidently
the Munchkins were good
farmers, able to raise large crops.
Once in a while she would pass a
house, and the people came out to
look at her and bow low as she went

by; for everyone knew she had been the means of destroying the Wicked Witch and setting them free from bondage. The Munchkin houses were odd-looking dwellings, for each was round, with a big dome for a roof. All were painted blue, for in this country of the East, blue was the favourite colour.

When she had gone several miles she thought she would stop to rest, and so climbed to the top of the fence beside the road and sat down. There was a great cornfield beyond the fence, and not far away she saw a Scarecrow, placed high on a pole to keep the birds from the ripe corn.

Dorothy leant her chin upon her hand and gazed at the Scarecrow. Its head was a small sack stuffed with straw, with eyes, nose, and mouth painted on it to represent a face. An old, pointed blue hat, that had belonged to some Munchkin, was perched on his head, and the rest of the figure was a blue suit of clothes, worn and faded, which had also been stuffed with straw. On the feet were some old boots with bluc tops, such as every man wore in this country, and the figure was raised above the stalks of corn by means of the pole stuck up its back.

While Dorothy was looking into the queer, painted face of the Scarecrow, she was surprised to see one of the eyes wink at her. She thought she must have been mistaken at first, for none of the scarecrows in Kansas ever wink; but presently the figure nodded its head to her in a friendly way. Then she climbed down from the fence and walked up to it, while Toto ran around the pole and barked.

"Good day," said the Scarecrow, in a husky voice.

"Did you speak?" asked the girl, in wonder.

"Certainly," answered the Scarecrow. "How do you do?"

"I'm pretty well, thank you," replied Dorothy politely. "How do you do?"

"I'm not feeling well," said the Scarecrow, with a smile, "for it is very tedious being perched up here night and day to scare away crows."

"Can't you get down?" asked Dorothy.

"No, for this pole is stuck up my back. If you will please take away the pole I shall be greatly obliged."

Dorothy reached up both arms and lifted the figure off the pole for, being stuffed with straw, it was quite light.

"Thank you very much," said the Scarecrow, when he had been set down on the ground. "I feel like a new man."

Dorothy was puzzled at this, for it sounded queer to hear a stuffed man speak, and to see him walk along beside her.

"Who are you?" asked the Scarecrow when he had stretched himself and yawned. "And where are you going?"

"My name is Dorothy," said the girl, "and I am going to the Emerald City, to ask the Great Oz to send me back to Kansas."

"Where is the Emerald City?" he inquired. "And who is Oz?"

"Why, don't you know?" she asked, in surprise.

"No, indeed – I don't know anything. You see, I am stuffed, so I have no brains at all," he answered her, sadly.

"Oh," said Dorothy, "I'm awfully sorry for you."

"Do you think," he asked, "if I go to the Emerald City with you, that the Great Oz would give me some brains?"

"I cannot tell," she returned, "but you may come with me, if you like. If Oz will not give you any brains you will be no worse off than you are now."

"That is true," said the Scarecrow. "You see," he continued confidentially, "I don't mind my legs and arms and body being stuffed, because I cannot get hurt. If anyone treads on my toes or sticks a pin into me, it doesn't matter, for I can't feel it. But I do not want people to call me a fool, and if my head stays stuffed with straw instead of with brains, how am I to know anything?"

"I understand how you feel," said the little girl,

who was truly sorry for him. "If you will come with me I'll ask Oz to do all he can for you."

"Thank you," he answered gratefully.

They walked back to the road. Dorothy helped him over the fence, and they started along the path of yellow brick.

Toto did not like this addition to the party at first. He smelled around the stuffed man as if he suspected there might be a nest of rats in the straw, and he often growled in a rather unfriendly way at the Scarecrow.

"Don't mind Toto," said Dorothy to her new friend. "He never bites."

"Oh, I'm not afraid," replied the Scarecrow. "He can't hurt the straw. Do let me carry that basket for you. I shall not mind it, for I can't get tired. I'll tell you a secret," he continued, as he walked along. "There is only one thing in the world I am afraid of."

"What is that?" asked Dorothy; "the Munchkin farmer who made you?"

"No," answered the Scarecrow; "it's fire."

After many hours of walking the light faded, and they found themselves stumbling along in the darkness. Dorothy could not see at all, but Toto could, and the Scarecrow declared he could see as well as by day. So she took hold of his arm and managed to get along fairly well.

"If you see any house, or any place where we can pass the night," she said, "you must tell me; for it is very uncomfortable walking in the dark."

Soon after the Scarecrow stopped. "I see a little cottage at the right of us," he said, "built of logs and branches. Shall we go there?"

"Yes, please," answered the child. "Indeed, I am all tired out."

So the Scarecrow led her through the trees until

they reached the cottage, and Dorothy entered and found a bed of dried leaves in one corner. She lay down at once, and with Toto beside her soon fell into a sound sleep. The Scarecrow, who was never tired, stood up in another corner and waited patiently until morning.

When Dorothy awoke the sun was shining through the trees and Toto had long been out chasing birds and squirrels. She sat up and looked around her. Scarecrow, still standing patiently in his corner, was waiting for her.

"We must go and search for water," she told him.

"Why do you want water?" he asked.

"To wash my face clean, and to drink, so the dry bread will not stick in my throat."

"It must be inconvenient to be made of flesh," said the Scarecrow, "for you must sleep, and eat and drink. However, you have brains, and it is worth a lot of bother to be able to think properly."

They left the cottage and walked through the

trees until they found a little spring of clear water, where Dorothy drank and bathed and ate her breakfast. She saw there was not much bread left in the basket, and the girl was thankful the Scarecrow did not have to eat anything, for there was scarcely enough for herself and Toto for the day.

When she had finished her meal, and was about start walking again, she was startled to hear a deep groan nearby.

"What was that?" she asked timidly.

"I cannot imagine," replied the Scarecrow; "but we can go and see."

Just then another groan reached their ears, and it seemed to come from behind them. They turned and walked through the forest a few steps, when Dorothy discovered something shining in a ray of sunshine that fell between the trees. She ran to the place and then stopped short, with a cry of surprise.

One of the big trees had been partly chopped through, and standing beside it, with an uplifted axe in his hands, was a man made entirely of tin. His head and arms and legs were jointed upon his body, but he stood motionless, as if he could not stir at all.

Dorothy looked at him in amazement, and so did the Scarecrow, while Toto barked sharply and made a snap at the tin legs, which hurt his teeth.

"Did you groan?" asked Dorothy.

"Yes," answered the tin man, "I've been groaning for more than a year. No one has heard me before."

"What can I do for you?" she inquired softly, for she was moved by the sad voice in which he spoke.

"Get an oil-can and oil my joints," he answered. "They are rusted so that I cannot move them at all; if I am well oiled I shall soon be all right again. You will find an oil-can on a shelf in my cottage."

Dorothy at once ran back to the cottage and found the oil-can, and then she returned and asked anxiously, "Where are your joints?"

"Oil my neck, first," replied the Tin Woodman. So she oiled it, and as it was quite badly rusted the

Scarecrow took hold of the tin head and moved it gently from side to side until it worked freely, and then the man could turn it himself.

"Now oil the joints in my arms," he said. And Dorothy oiled them and the Scarecrow bent them carefully until they were as good as new.

The Tin Woodman gave a sigh of satisfaction and lowered his axe, leaning it against the tree. "This is a great comfort," he said. "I have been holding that axe in the air since I rusted. I'm glad to be able to put it down at last. Now, if you will oil the joints of my legs, I shall be all right once more."

So they oiled his legs until he could move them freely; and he thanked them again for his release. "I might have stood there always if you had not come along," he said; "so you have certainly saved my life. How did you happen to be here?"

"We are on our way to the Emerald City to see the Great Oz," she answered, "and we stopped at your cottage to pass the night."

"Why do you wish to see Oz?" he asked.

"I want him to send me back to Kansas, and the Scarecrow wants him to put a few brains into his head," she replied.

The Tin Woodman said, "Do you suppose Oz could give me a heart?"

"Why, I guess so," Dorothy answered. "It would be as easy as to give the Scarecrow brains."

"True," the Tin Woodman returned. "So, if you will allow me to join your party, I will also go to the Emerald City and ask Oz to help me."

"Come along," said the Scarecrow heartily, and Dorothy added that she would be pleased to have his company. So the Tin Woodman shouldered his axe and they all passed through the forest until they came to the road paved with yellow brick.

The Tin Woodman asked Dorothy to put the oil-can in her basket. "For," he said, "if I should get caught in the rain, I would need the oil-can badly."

It was a bit of good luck to have their new

comrade, for soon after they had begun their journey again they came to a place where the trees and branches grew so thick over the road that the travellers could not pass. But the Tin Woodman set to work with his axe and chopped so well that soon he cleared a passage for the entire party.

Dorothy was thinking so earnestly as they walked along that she did not notice when the Scarecrow stumbled into a hole. Indeed he was obliged to call to her to help him up again.

greatly interested in the story of the Tin Woodman, and now they knew why he was so anxious to get a new heart. "All the same," said the Scarecrow, "I shall ask for brains; for a fool would not know what to do with a heart if he had one."

"I shall take the heart," returned the Tin Woodman; "for brains do not make one happy, and happiness is the best thing in the world."

Dorothy did not say anything, for she was puzzled to know which of her two friends was right. What worried her most was that the bread was nearly gone, and another meal for herself and Toto would empty the basket.

All this time Dorothy and her companions had been walking through the thick woods. The road was still paved with yellow brick, but these were much covered by dried branches and dead leaves from the trees, and the walking was not at all good.

There were few birds in this part of the forest, but now and then there came a deep growl from some wild animal hidden among the trees. These sounds made the little girl's heart beat fast, for she did not know what made them; but Toto knew, and he walked close to Dorothy's side, and did not even bark in return.

"How long will it be," the child asked of the Tin Woodman, "before we are out of the forest?"

"I cannot tell," was the answer, "for I have never been to the Emerald City. But my father went there once, when I was a boy, and he said it was a long journey through a dangerous country, although nearer to the city where Oz dwells the country is beautiful. But I am not afraid so long as I have my oil-can, and nothing can hurt the Scarecrow, while you have been kissed by the Good Witch, and that will protect you from harm."

"But Toto!" said the girl anxiously. "What will protect him?"

"We must protect him ourselves if he is in danger," replied the Tin Woodman.

Just as he spoke there came from the forest a terrible roar, and the next moment a great Lion bounded into the road. With a blow of his paw he sent the Scarecrow spinning over to the edge of the road, and then he struck at the Tin Woodman with his sharp claws. But, to the Lion's surprise, he could make no impression on the tin, although the Woodman fell over in the road and lay still.

Little Toto ran barking toward the Lion, and the great beast had opened his mouth to bite the dog, when Dorothy, fearing Toto would be killed, and heedless of danger, rushed forward and slapped the Lion upon his nose as hard as she could, crying out: "Don't you dare to bite Toto! You ought to be ashamed of yourself, a big beast like you, to bite a poor little dog!"

"I didn't bite him," said the Lion, as he rubbed his nose with his paw where Dorothy had hit it.

"No, but you tried to," she retorted. "You are nothing but a big coward."

"I know it," said the Lion, hanging his head in shame. "But how can I help it?"

"I don't know, I'm sure. To think of your striking a stuffed man, like the poor Scarecrow!"

"Is he stuffed?" asked the Lion in surprise, as he watched her pick up the Scarecrow and set him upon his feet, while she patted him into shape.

"Of course he's stuffed," replied Dorothy, who was still angry.

"That's why he went over so easily," remarked the

Lion. "It astonished me to see him whirl around so. Is the other one stuffed also?"

"No," said Dorothy, "he's made of tin." And she helped the Woodman up again.

"That's why he nearly blunted my claws," said the Lion. "When they scratched against the tin it made a cold shiver run down my back. What is that little animal you are so tender of?"

"He is my dog, Toto," answered Dorothy.

"Is he made of tin, or stuffed?" asked the Lion.

"Neither. He's a – a meat dog," said the girl.

"Oh! He's a curious animal and seems remarkably small, now that I look at him. No one would think of biting such a little thing, except a coward like me," continued the Lion sadly.

"What makes you a coward?" asked Dorothy.

"It's a mystery," replied the Lion. "All the other animals in the forest naturally expect me to be brave. I learnt that if I roared very loudly every living thing was frightened and got out of my way.

Whenever I've met a man I've been awfully scared; but I just roared at him, and he has always run away. If the elephants and the tigers and the bears had ever tried to fight me, I should have run myself; but as soon as they hear me roar they try to get away from me, and of course I let them go."

"But that isn't right. The 'king of beasts' shouldn't be a coward," said the Scarecrow.

"I know," returned the Lion, wiping a tear from his eye with the tip of his tail. "It is my great sorrow, and makes my life very unhappy. But whenever there is danger, my heart begins to beat fast."

"Perhaps you have heart disease," suggested the Tin Woodman.

"It may be," said the Lion.

"If you have," continued the Tin Woodman, "it proves you have a heart. I have no heart."

"Perhaps," said the Lion thoughtfully, "if I had no heart I should not be a coward."

"Have you brains?" asked the Scarecrow.

"I suppose so. I've never looked to see," replied the Lion.

"I am going to the Great Oz to ask him to give me some," remarked the Scarecrow.

"And I am going to ask him to give me a heart," said the Woodman.

"And I am going to ask him to send Toto and me back to Kansas," added Dorothy.

"Do you think Oz could give me courage?" asked the Cowardly Lion.

"Just as easily as he could give me brains," said the Scarecrow.

"Or give me a heart," said the Tin Woodman.

"Or send me back to Kansas," said Dorothy.

"Then, if you don't mind, I'll go with you," said the Lion, "for my life is simply unbearable without a bit of courage."

"You will be very welcome," answered Dorothy, "for you will help to keep away the other wild beasts. It seems to me they must be more cowardly than you are if they allow you to scare them."

"They really are," said the Lion, "but that doesn't make me any braver, and as long as I know myself to be a coward I shall be unhappy."

So once more the little company set off upon the journey, the Lion walking with stately strides at Dorothy's side. Toto did not approve of this new comrade at first, for he could not forget how nearly he had been crushed between the Lion's great jaws. But after a time he became more at ease, and presently Toto and the Cowardly Lion had grown to be good friends.

SECRETS
REVEALED

Down the Rabbit-hole

From *Alice's Adventures in Wonderland*
by Lewis Carroll

Alice was beginning to get very tired of sitting by her sister on the bank, and of having nothing to do. Once or twice she had peeped into the book her sister was reading, but it had no pictures or conversations in it. 'And what is the use of a book,' thought Alice, 'without pictures or conversation?'

So she was considering (as well as she could, for the hot day made her feel very sleepy and stupid) whether the pleasure of making a daisy-chain would be worth the trouble of getting up and picking the daisies, when suddenly a White Rabbit with pink eyes ran close by her.

There was nothing so very remarkable in that. Nor did Alice think it so very much out of the way to hear the Rabbit say to itself, "Oh dear! Oh dear! I shall be late!" (When she thought it over afterwards, it occurred to her that she ought to have wondered at this, but at the time it all seemed quite natural.) When the Rabbit actually took a watch out of its waistcoat-pocket, looked at it, and then hurried on, Alice started to her feet, for it flashed across her mind that she had never seen a rabbit with either a waistcoat-pocket or a watch to take out of it. Burning with curiosity, she ran across the field after it, and fortunately was just in time to see it pop down a large rabbit-hole under the hedge.

In another moment down went Alice after it. The rabbit-hole went straight on like a tunnel for some way, and then dipped suddenly down, so that Alice had not a moment to think about stopping herself before she found herself falling down a well.

First, she tried to look down and make out what she was coming to, but it was too dark to see anything. Then she looked at the sides of the well, and she noticed that they were filled with cupboards and bookshelves. Here and there she saw maps and pictures hung upon pegs. She took down a jar from one of the shelves as she passed. It was labelled orange marmalade, but to her great disappointment it was empty. She did not like to drop the jar for fear of killing somebody, so managed to put it into one of the cupboards as she fell past it.

'Well!' thought Alice to herself. 'After such a fall as this, I shall think nothing of tumbling down stairs! How brave they'll all think me at home! Why, I wouldn't say anything about it, even if I fell off the top of the house!'

Down, down, down. Would the fall never come to an end? "I wonder how many miles I've fallen by

this time?" she said aloud. "I must be getting somewhere near the centre of the earth. Let me see, that would be four thousand miles down, I think…" (For, you see, Alice had learnt several things of this sort in her lessons in the schoolroom, and though this was not a very good opportunity for showing off her knowledge, as there was no one to listen to her, still it was good practice to say it over.)

"Yes, that's about the right distance – but then I wonder what latitude or longitude I've got to?" (Alice had no idea what latitude was, or longitude either, but thought they were nice grand words to say.)

Presently she began again. "I wonder if I shall fall right through the earth! How funny it'll seem to come out among the people that walk with their heads downward! But I shall have to ask them what the name of the country is, you know. Please, Ma'am, is this New Zealand or Australia?" (And she tried to curtsey as she spoke – fancy curtseying as you're falling through the air! Do you think you could manage it?) "And what an ignorant little girl she'll think me for asking! No, it'll never do to ask, but perhaps I shall see it written up somewhere."

Down, down, down. There was nothing else to do, so Alice soon began talking again. "Dinah'll miss me very much tonight, I should think!" (Dinah was the cat.) "I hope they'll remember her saucer of milk at tea-time. Dinah my dear! I wish you were down here with me! There are no mice in the air, I'm afraid, but you might catch a bat, and that's very like a mouse, you know. But do cats eat bats, I wonder?"

Alice began to get rather sleepy, and went on saying to herself, in a dreamy sort of way, "Do cats eat bats?" and sometimes, "Do bats eat cats?" (For, you see, as she couldn't answer either question, it didn't much matter which way she put it.)

She felt that she was dozing off, and had just begun to dream that she was walking hand in hand with Dinah, and saying to her earnestly, "Now, Dinah, tell me the truth: did you ever eat a bat?" when suddenly, *thump!* Down she came upon a heap of sticks and dry leaves, and the fall was over.

Alice was not a bit hurt, and she jumped up on to her feet in a moment. She looked up, but it was all dark overhead. Before her was another long passage, and the White Rabbit was still in sight,

hurrying down it. There was not a moment to be lost: away went Alice like the wind, and was just in time to hear it say, as it turned a corner, "Oh my ears and whiskers, how late it's getting!"

She was close behind it when she turned the corner, but the Rabbit was no longer to be seen. She found herself in a long, low hall, which was lit up by a row of lamps hanging from the roof.

There were doors all round the hall, but they were all locked, and when Alice had been all the way down one side and up the other, trying every door, she walked sadly down the middle, wondering how she was ever to get out again…

The Terrible Secret

From *The Railway Children*
by E Nesbit

Roberta (Bobbie), Peter and Phyllis have to move to the country with their mother when their father is suddenly taken away. The children spend much of their time watching the trains that pass by their cottage.

When they first went to live at Three Chimneys, the children had talked a great deal about their Father, and had asked a great many questions about him, and what he was doing and where he was and when he would come home. Mother always answered their questions as well as she could. But as the time went on they grew to speak less of him.

The Terrible Secret

Bobbie had felt almost from the first that for some strange miserable reason these questions hurt Mother and made her sad. And little by little the others came to have this feeling, too, though they could not have put it into words.

One day, when Mother was working so hard that she could not leave off even for ten minutes, Bobbie carried up her tea to the big bare room that they called Mother's workshop. It had hardly any furniture. Just a table and a chair and a rug. But always big pots of flowers on the window-sills and on the mantelpiece. The children saw to that. And from the three long uncurtained windows the beautiful stretch of meadow and moorland, the far violet of the hills, and the unchanging changefulness of cloud and sky.

"Here's your tea, Mother-love," said Bobbie. "Do drink it while it's hot."

Mother laid down her pen among the pages that were scattered all over the table, pages covered with her writing, which was almost as plain as print, and much prettier. She ran her hands into her hair, as if she were going to pull it out by handfuls.

"Poor dear head," said Bobbie, "does it ache?"

"No – yes – not much," said Mother. "Bobbie, do you think Peter and Phil are forgetting Father?"

"No," said Bobbie, indignantly. "Why?"

"You none of you ever speak of him now."

Bobbie stood first on one leg and then on the other as she thought how to reply.

"We often talk about him when we're by ourselves," she said.

"But not to me," said Mother. "Why?"

Bobbie did not find it easy to say why. "I – you—" she said and stopped. She went over to the window and looked out.

"Bobbie, come here," said her Mother, and Bobbie came.

"Now," said Mother with a gentle smile, putting her arm round Bobbie and laying her ruffled head

against Bobbie's shoulder, "do try to tell me, dear."

Bobbie fidgeted.

"Tell Mother."

"Well, then," said Bobbie, "I thought you were so unhappy about Daddy not being here, it made you worse when I talked about him. So I stopped."

"And the others?"

"I don't know about the others," said Bobbie. "I never said anything about that to them. But I expect they felt the same about it as me."

"Bobbie dear," said Mother, still leaning her head against her, "I'll tell you. Besides parting from Father, he and I have had a great sorrow – oh, terrible – worse than anything you can think of, and at first it did hurt to hear you all talking of him as if everything were just the same. But it would be much more terrible if you were to forget him. That would be worse than anything."

"The trouble," said Bobbie, in a very little voice, "I promised I would never ask you any questions,

and I never have, have I? But – the trouble – it
won't last always?"

"No," said Mother, "the worst will be over when
Father comes home to us."

"I wish I could comfort you," said Bobbie.

"Oh, my dear, do you suppose you don't? Do you
think I haven't noticed how good you've all been,
not quarrelling nearly as much as you used to – and
all the little kind things you do for me – the flowers,
and cleaning my shoes, and tearing up to make my
bed before I get time to do it myself?"

Bobbie had sometimes wondered whether
Mother noticed these things.

"That's nothing," she said, "to what—"

"I must get on with my work," said Mother,
giving Bobbie one last squeeze. "Don't say anything
to the others."

That evening in the hour before bedtime
instead of reading to the children Mother told them
stories of the games she and Father used to have

The Terrible Secret

when they were children and lived near each other in the country – tales of the adventures of Father with Mother's brothers when they were all boys together. Very funny stories they were, and the children laughed as they listened.

"Uncle Edward died before he was grown up, didn't he?" said Phyllis, as Mother lighted the bedroom candles.

"Yes, dear," said Mother, "you would have loved him. He was such a brave boy, and so adventurous. Always in mischief, and yet friends with everybody in spite of it. And your Uncle Reggie's in Ceylon, and Father's away, too. But I think they'd all like to think we'd enjoyed talking about the things they used to do. Don't you think so?"

"Not Uncle Edward," said Phyllis, in a shocked tone, "he's in heaven."

"You don't suppose he's forgotten us and all the old times, because God has taken him, any more than I forget him. Oh, no, he remembers. He's only away for a little time. We shall see him some day."

"And Uncle Reggie – and Father, too?" said Peter, softly.

"Yes," said Mother. "Uncle Reggie and Father, too. Good night, my darlings."

"Good night," said everyone. When it was her turn, Bobbie hugged her mother more closely even than usual, and whispered in her ear, "Oh, I do love you so, Mummy – I do – I do—"

When Bobbie came to think it all over, she tried not to wonder what the great trouble was. But she could not always help it. Father was not dead – like poor Uncle Edward – Mother had said so. And he was not ill, or Mother would have been with him. Being poor wasn't the trouble. Bobbie knew it was something nearer the heart than money could be.

"I mustn't try to think what it is," she told herself, "no, I mustn't. I am glad Mother noticed about us not quarrelling so much. We'll keep that up." But alas, that very afternoon she and Peter had what Peter called a first-class shindy.

They had not been a week at Three Chimneys before they had asked Mother to let them have a piece of garden each for their very own, and she had agreed, and the south border under the peach trees had been divided into three pieces and they were allowed to plant whatever they liked there.

Phyllis had planted mignonette and nasturtium

and Virginia Stock in hers. The seeds came up, and though they looked just like weeds, Phyllis believed that they would bear flowers some day. The Virginia Stock justified her faith quite soon, and her garden was bright with a band of vivid little flowers, pink and white and red and mauve.

"I can't weed for fear I pull up the wrong things," she used to say comfortably, "it saves a lot of work."

Peter sowed vegetable seeds in his – carrots and onions and turnips. The seed was given to him by the farmer who lived in the nice black-and-white, wood-and-plaster house just beyond the bridge. He kept turkeys and guinea fowls, and was a most amiable man. But Peter's vegetables never had much of a chance, because he liked to use the earth of his garden for digging canals, and making forts and earthworks for his toy soldiers. And the seeds of vegetables rarely come to much in a soil that is constantly being disturbed for the purposes of war and irrigation.

The Terrible Secret

Bobbie planted rose-bushes in her garden, but all the little new leaves of the rose-bushes shrivelled and withered, perhaps because she moved them from the other part of the garden in May, which is not at all the right time of year for moving roses. But she would not own that they were dead, until the day when Perks came up to see the garden, and told her quite plainly that all her roses were as dead as doornails.

"They're only good for bonfires, Miss," he said. "You just dig 'em up and burn 'em, and I'll give you some nice fresh roots outer my garden – pansies, and stocks, and sweet willies, and forget-me-nots. I'll bring 'em all along tomorrow if you get the ground ready."

So next day she set to work, and that happened to be the day when Mother had praised her and the others about not quarrelling. She moved the rose-bushes and carried them to the other end of the garden, where the rubbish heap was that they

planned to make into a bonfire of when Guy
Fawkes' Day came.

Meanwhile Peter had decided to flatten out all
his forts and earthworks, with a view to making a
model of the railway-tunnel, cutting, embankment,
canal, aqueduct, bridges and all.

So when Bobbie came back from her last thorny
journey with the dead rose-bushes, he had got the
rake and was using it busily.

"I was using the rake," said Bobbie.

"Well, I'm using it now," said Peter.

"But I had it first," said Bobbie.

"Then it's my turn now," said Peter.
And that was how the quarrel began.
"You're always being disagreeable
about nothing," said Peter, after some
heated argument.

"I had the rake first," said Bobbie,
flushed and defiant, holding onto
its handle.

"Don't – I tell you I said this morning I meant to have it. Didn't I, Phil?"

Phyllis said she didn't want to be mixed up in their rows. And instantly, of course, she was.

"If you remember, you ought to say."

"Of course she doesn't remember – but she might say so."

"I wish I'd had a brother instead of two whiny little kiddy sisters," said Peter. This was always recognized as indicating the high-water mark of Peter's rage.

Bobbie made the reply she always made to it.

"I can't think why little boys were ever invented," and just as she said it she

looked up, and saw the three long windows of
Mother's workshop flashing in the red rays of the
sun. The sight brought back those words of praise:
'You don't quarrel like you used to do.'"

"Oh!" cried Bobbie, just as if she had been hit, or
had caught her finger in a door, or had felt the
hideous sharp beginnings of toothache.

"What's the matter?" said Phyllis.

Bobbie wanted to say: 'Don't let's quarrel.
Mother hates it so,' but she couldn't. Peter was
looking too disagreeable and insulting.

"Take the horrid rake, then," was the best she
could manage. And she suddenly let go her hold on
the handle. Peter had been holding on to it too
firmly, and now that the pull the other way was
suddenly stopped, he staggered and fell over
backward, the teeth of the rake between his feet.

"Serve you right," said Bobbie, before she could
stop herself.

Peter lay still for half a moment – long enough to

frighten Bobbie a little. Then he frightened her a little more, for he sat up, screamed once, turned rather pale, and then lay back and began to shriek, faintly but steadily. It sounded exactly like a pig being killed a quarter of a mile off.

Mother put her head out of the window, and it wasn't half a minute after that she was in the garden kneeling by the side of Peter, who never for an instant ceased to squeal.

"What happened, Bobbie?" Mother asked.

"It was because of the rake," said Phyllis. "Peter was pulling at it, so was Bobbie, and she let go and he went over."

"Stop that noise, Peter," said Mother. "Come. Stop at once."

Peter used up what breath he had left in a last squeal and stopped.

"Now," said Mother, "are you hurt?"

"He must be really hurt, or he wouldn't make such a fuss," said Bobbie, still trembling with fury but feeling scared, "he's not a coward!"

"I think my foot's broken off, that's all," said Peter, huffily, and sat up. Then he turned quite white. Mother put her arm round him.

"He is hurt," she said, "he's fainted. Here, Bobbie, sit down and take his head on your lap."

Then Mother undid Peter's boots. As she took the right one off, red blood dripped from his foot on to the ground. And when the stocking came off there were three red wounds in Peter's foot and ankle, where the teeth of the rake had bitten him, and his foot was covered with red smears.

"Run for water – a basinful," said Mother, and Phyllis ran. She upset most of the water out of the basin in her haste, and had to fetch more in a jug.

Peter did not open his eyes again till Mother had tied her handkerchief round his foot, and she and Bobbie had carried him in and laid him on the brown wooden settle in the dining room. By this time Phyllis was halfway to the Doctor's.

The Terrible Secret

Mother sat by Peter and bathed his foot and talked to him, and Bobbie went out and got tea ready, and put on the kettle.

'It's all I can do,' she thought to herself. 'Oh, suppose Peter should die, or be a helpless cripple for life, or have to walk with crutches, or wear a boot with a sole like a log of wood!' She stood by the back door reflecting on these gloomy possibilities, her eyes fixed on the water-butt.

"I wish I'd never been born," she said, and she said it out loud.

The Doctor came and looked at the foot and bandaged it beautifully, and said that Peter must not put it to the ground for at least a week.

"He won't be lame, or have to wear crutches or have a lump on his foot, will he?" whispered Bobbie, breathlessly, at the door.

"My aunt! No!" said Dr Forrest, "he'll be as nimble as ever on his pins in a fortnight. Don't you worry, little Mother Goose."

It was when Mother had gone to the gate with the Doctor to take his last instructions and Phyllis was filling the kettle for tea, that Peter and Bobbie found themselves alone.

"He says you won't be lame," said Bobbie.

"Oh, course I shan't, silly," said Peter, very much relieved all the same.

"Oh, Peter, I am sorry," said Bobbie, after a pause.

"That's all right," said Peter, gruffly.

"It was all my fault," said Bobbie.

"Rot," said Peter.

"If we hadn't quarrelled, it wouldn't have happened. I knew it was wrong to quarrel. I wanted to say so, but somehow I couldn't."

"Don't drivel," said Peter. "I shouldn't have stopped if you had said it. Not likely."

"But I knew it was wrong to quarrel," said Bobbie, in tears, "and now you're hurt and—"

"Now look here," said Peter, firmly, "you just dry up. If you're not careful, you'll turn into a beastly little Sunday-school prig, so I tell you."

"I don't mean to be a prig. But it's so hard not to be when you're really trying to be good."

"Not it," said Peter, "it's a jolly good thing it wasn't you that was hurt. I'm glad it was me. There! If it had been you, you'd have been lying on the sofa looking like a suffering angel and being the light of the anxious household and all that. And I couldn't have stood it."

"No, I shouldn't," said Bobbie.

"Yes, you would," said Peter.

"I tell you I shouldn't."

"I tell you you would."

"Oh, children," said Mother's voice at the door.

"Quarrelling again? Already?"

"We aren't quarrelling – not really," said Peter. "I wish you wouldn't think it's rows every time we don't agree!"

When Mother had gone out again, Bobbie broke out, "Peter, I am sorry you're hurt. But you are a beast to say I'm a prig."

"Well," said Peter unexpectedly, "perhaps I am. You did say I wasn't a coward, even when you were in such a wax. The only thing is – don't you be a prig, that's all. You keep your eyes open and if you feel priggishness coming on just stop in time. See?"

"Yes," said Bobbie, "I see."

"Then let's call it Pax," said Peter, magnanimously. "Bury the hatchet. I say, Bobbie, old chap, I am tired."

At first Bobbie found it quite hard to be as nice to him as she wanted to be, for fear he should think her priggish. But that soon wore off, and both she and Phyllis were, as he observed, jolly good sorts.

The Terrible Secret

Mother sat with him when his sisters were out. And the words, 'he's not a coward,' made Peter determined not to fuss about the pain in his foot, though it was rather bad. Praise helps people very much, sometimes.

There were visitors, too. Mrs Perks came up to ask how he was, and so did the Station Master, and several of the village people. But the time went slowly, slowly.

"I do wish there was something to read," said Peter. "I've read all our books fifty times over."

"I'll go to the Doctor's," said Phyllis, "he's sure to have some."

"Only about how to be ill, and about people's nasty insides, I expect," said Peter.

"Perks has a whole heap of magazines that came out of trains when people are tired of them," said Bobbie. "I'll run down and ask him." So the girls went their two ways.

Bobbie found Perks busy cleaning lamps. "And

how's the young gent?" he asked.

"Better, thanks," said Bobbie, "but he's most frightfully bored. I came to ask if you'd got any magazines you could lend him."

"There, now," said Perks, regretfully, "why didn't I think of that? I was trying to think of something as 'ud amuse him only this morning, and I couldn't think of anything better than a guinea-pig. And a young chap I know's going to fetch that over for him this teatime."

"How lovely! A real live guinea! He will be pleased. But he'd like the magazines as well."

"That's just it," said Perks. "I've sent the pick of 'em to Snigson's boy – him what's just getting over the pewmonia. But I've lots of illustrated papers."

He turned to the pile of papers in the corner and took up a heap six inches thick.

"There!" he said. "I'll just slip a bit of string and a bit of paper round 'em."

He pulled an old newspaper from the pile and

spread it on the table, and made a neat parcel of it.

"There," said he, "there's lots of pictures, and if he likes to mess 'em about with his paint-box, or coloured chalks or what not, why, let him. I don't want 'em."

"You're a dear," said Bobbie. She took the parcel and set off for home. The papers were heavy, and when she had to wait at the level-crossing while a train went by, she rested the parcel on the top of the gate. And idly she looked at the printing on the paper that the parcel was wrapped in.

Suddenly she clutched the parcel tighter and bent her head over it. It seemed like some horrible dream. She read on – the bottom of the column was torn off – she could read no farther.

She never remembered how she got home. But she went on tiptoe to her room and locked the door. Then she undid the parcel and read that column again, sitting on the edge of her bed. When she had read all there was, she drew a long breath.

"So now I know," she said. What she had read was headed, 'End of the Trial. Verdict. Sentence.'

The name of the man who had been tried was the name of her Father. The verdict was 'Guilty.' And the sentence was 'Five years' Penal Servitude.'

"Oh, Daddy," she whispered, crushing the paper hard, "it's not true – I don't believe it. You never did it! Never, never, never!"

There was a hammering on the door.

"What is it?" said Bobbie.

"It's me," said the voice of Phyllis; "it's time for tea, and a boy's brought Peter a guinea-pig. Come along down."

And Bobbie had to.

The Banquet Lamp

From *Rebecca of Sunnybrook Farm*
by Kate Douglas Wiggin

Rebecca is sent to live with her two unmarried aunts.
She and her friends have been selling soap in order to try and
win the 'banquet lamp' – a tall elaborate table lamp – that the
soap company are giving away as a reward for sales.

There had been company at the brick house to the bountiful Thanksgiving dinner that had been provided at one o'clock – the Burnham sisters, who lived between North Riverboro and Shaker Village, and who for more than a quarter of a century had come to pass the holiday with the

Sawyers every year. Rebecca sat silent with a book
after the dinner dishes were washed, and after what
felt like many hours – when it was nearly five –
asked if she might go to the Simpsons'.

"What do you want to run after those Simpson
children for on a Thanksgiving Day?" queried
Miss Miranda. "Can't you set still for once and
listen to the improvin' conversation of your elders?
You never can let well enough alone, but want to be
forever on the move."

"The Simpsons have a new lamp, and Emma Jane
and I promised to go up and see it lighted, and
make it a kind of a party."

"What under the canopy did they want of a
lamp, and where did they get the money to pay for
it? If Abner was at home, I should think he'd been
swappin' again," said Miss Miranda.

"The children got it as a prize for selling soap,"
replied Rebecca. "They've been working for a year,
and you know I told you that Emma Jane and I

helped them the Saturday afternoon you were in Portland."

"I didn't take notice, I s'pose, for it's the first time I ever heard the lamp mentioned. Well, you can go for an hour, and no more. Remember it's as dark at six as it is at midnight. Would you like to take along some Baldwin apples? And what have you got in the pocket of that new dress that is making it sag down so?"

"It's my nuts and raisins from dinner," replied Rebecca, who never succeeded in keeping the most innocent action a secret from her aunt Miranda. "They're just what you gave me on my plate."

"Why didn't you eat them?"

"Because I'd had enough dinner, and I thought if I saved these, it would make the Simpsons' party better," stammered Rebecca, who hated to be scolded and examined before company.

"They were your own, Rebecca," interposed aunt Jane, "and if you chose to save them to give away, it is all right. We ought never to let this day pass without giving our neighbours something to be thankful for, instead of taking all the time to think of our own mercies."

The Burnham sisters nodded approvingly as Rebecca went out, and remarked that they had never seen a child grow and improve so fast in so short a time.

"There's plenty of room left for more improvement, as you'd know if she lived in the same house with you," answered Miranda. "She's into every namable thing in the neighbourhood, an' not only into it, but generally at the head an' front of it – especially when it's mischief. Of all the foolishness I ever heard of, that lamp beats everything; it's just like those Simpsons, but I didn't suppose any of those children had brains enough to sell anything."

"One of them must have," said Miss Ellen Burnham, "for the girl that was selling soap at the

Ladds' in North Riverboro was described by
Adam Ladd as the most remarkable and winning
child he ever saw."

"It must have been Clara Belle, and I should
never call her remarkable," answered Miss Miranda.
"Has Adam been home again?"

"Yes, he's been staying a few days with his aunt.
There's no limit to the money he's making, they
say; and he always brings presents for all the
neighbours. This time it was a full set of furs for
Mrs Ladd – and to think we can remember the time
he was a barefoot boy without two shirts to his
back! It is strange he hasn't married, with all his
money, and him so fond of children that he always
has a pack of them at his heels."

"There's hope for him still, though," said
Miss Jane smilingly. "I don't s'pose he can be more
than thirty."

"He could get a wife in Riverboro if he was a
hundred and thirty," remarked Miss Miranda.

"Adam's aunt says he was so taken with the little girl that sold the soap – Clara Belle, did you say her name was? – that he declared he was going to bring her a Christmas present," continued Miss Ellen.

"Well, there's no accountin' for tastes," exclaimed Miss Miranda. "Clara Belle's got cross-eyes and red hair, but I'd be the last one to grudge her a Christmas present – the more Adam Ladd gives to her the less the town'll have to."

"Isn't there another Simpson girl?" asked Miss Lydia Burnham; "For this one couldn't have been cross-eyed – I remember Mrs Ladd saying Adam remarked about this child's handsome eyes. He said it was her eyes that made him buy the three hundred cakes. Mrs Ladd has it stacked up in the shed chamber."

"Three hundred cakes!" cried Miranda. "Well, as always, there's one crop for sure that never fails in Riverboro!"

"What's that?" asked Miss Lydia politely.

The Banquet Lamp

"The fool crop," responded Miranda tersely, and changed the subject, much to Jane's gratitude, for she had been nervous and ill at ease for the last fifteen minutes. What child in Riverboro could be described as remarkable and winning, save Rebecca? What child had wonderful eyes, except the same Rebecca? And finally, was there ever a child in the world who could make a man buy soap by the hundred cakes, save Rebecca?

Meantime the 'remarkable' child had flown up the road in the deepening dusk, but she had not gone far before she heard the sound of hurrying footsteps, and saw a well-known figure coming in her direction. In a moment she and Emma Jane met and exchanged a breathless embrace.

"Something awful has happened with the lamp," panted Emma Jane.

"Don't tell me it's broken," exclaimed Rebecca.

"No! Oh, no! Not that! It was packed in straw, and every piece came out all right; and I was there. And I never said a single thing about your selling the three hundred cakes that got the lamp, so that we could be together when you told."

"Our selling the three hundred cakes," corrected Rebecca; "You did as much as I."

"No, I didn't, Rebecca Randall. I just sat at the gate and held the horse."

"Yes, but whose horse was it that took us to North Riverboro? And besides, it just happened to be my turn. If you had gone in and found Mr Aladdin you would have had the wonderful lamp given to you. But what's the trouble?"

"The Simpsons have no kerosene and no wicks. I guess they thought a banquet lamp was something that lighted itself, and burnt without any help.

The Banquet Lamp

Seesaw has gone to the doctor's to try if he can borrow a wick, and mother let me have a pint of oil, but she says she won't give me any more. We never even thought of the expense of keeping up the lamp, Rebecca."

"No, we didn't, but let's not worry about that till after the party. I have a handful of nuts and raisins and some apples."

"I have peppermints and maple sugar," said Emma Jane. "They had a real Thanksgiving dinner; the doctor gave them sweet potatoes and cranberries and turnips; father sent a spare-rib, and Mrs Cobb a chicken and a jar of mince-meat."

At half past five one might have looked in at the Simpsons' windows, and seen the party at its height. Mrs Simpson had let the kitchen fire die out, and had brought the baby to grace the festive scene. The lamp seemed to be having the party, and receiving the guests. The children had taken the one small table in the house, and it was placed in the far

corner of the room to serve as a pedestal. On it stood the sacred, the adored, the long-desired object; almost as beautiful, and nearly half as large as the advertisement. The brass glistened like gold, and the crimson paper shade glowed like a giant ruby. In the wide splash of light that it flung upon the floor sat the Simpsons, in reverent and

solemn silence, Emma Jane standing behind them, hand in hand with Rebecca. There seemed to be no desire for conversation – the occasion was too thrilling and serious for that. The lamp, it was tacitly felt by everybody, was dignifying the party, and providing sufficient entertainment simply by its presence; being fully as satisfactory in its way as a pianola or a string band.

"I wish that father could see it," whispered Clara Belle loyally.

"If he onth thaw it he'd want to thwap it," murmured Susan sagaciously.

At the appointed hour Rebecca dragged herself reluctantly away from the enchanting scene.

"I'll turn the lamp out the minute I think you and Emma Jane are home," said Clara Belle. "And I'm so glad you both live where you can see it shine. I wonder how long it will burn without bein' filled if I only keep it lit one hour every night?"

"You needn't put it out for want o' kerosene,' said

Seesaw, coming in from the shed, 'for there's a great keg of it settin' out there. Mr Tubbs brought it over from North Riverboro and said somebody sent an order by mail for it."

Rebecca squeezed Emma Jane's arm, and Emma Jane gave a rapturous return squeeze.

"It was Mr Aladdin," whispered Rebecca, as they ran down the path to the gate.

Rebecca entered the home dining room joyously. The Burnham sisters had gone and the two aunts were knitting.

"It was a heavenly party," she cried, taking off her hat and cape.

"Go back and see if you have shut the door tight, and then lock it," said Miss Miranda, in her usual austere manner.

"It was a heavenly party," reiterated Rebecca, coming in again, much too excited to be easily crushed. "And oh! aunt Jane, aunt Miranda, if you'll only come into the kitchen and look out of the sink window, you can see the banquet lamp shining all red, just as if the Simpsons' house was on fire."

"And probably it will be before long," observed Miranda. "I've got no patience with such foolish goin's on."

Jane accompanied Rebecca into the kitchen. Although the glimmer that she was able to see from that distance did not seem to her a dazzling exhibition, she tried to be enthusiastic.

"Rebecca, who was it that sold the three hundred cakes of soap to Mr Ladd in North Riverboro?"

"Mr Who?" exclaimed Rebecca

"Mr Ladd, in North Riverboro."

"Is that his real name?" queried Rebecca in astonishment. "I didn't make a bad guess," and she laughed softly to herself.

"I asked you who sold the soap to Adam Ladd?" resumed Miss Jane.

"Adam Ladd! then he's 'A. Ladd' – what fun!"

"Answer me, Rebecca."

"Oh! excuse me, aunt Jane, I was busy thinking. Emma Jane and I sold the soap to Mr Ladd."

"Did you tease him, or make him buy it?"

"Now, aunt Jane, how could I make a big grown-up man buy anything if he didn't want to? He needed the soap dreadfully he said, as a present for his aunt."

Miss Jane still looked a little unconvinced, though she only said, "I hope your aunt Miranda won't mind, but you know how particular she is, Rebecca, and I really wish you wouldn't do anything out of the ordinary without asking her first, for your actions are very strange."

"There can't be anything wrong this time," Rebecca answered confidently. "Emma Jane sold her cakes to her own relations and to uncle Jerry Cobb, and I went first to those new tenements near the lumber mill, and then to the Ladds'. Mr Ladd bought all we had and made us promise to keep the secret until the premium came, and I've been going about ever since then as if the banquet lamp was inside of me all lighted up and burning, for everybody to see."

Rebecca's hair was loosened and falling over her forehead in ruffled waves; her eyes were brilliant, her cheeks crimson; there was a hint of everything in the girl's face – of sensitiveness and delicacy as well as of ardour; there was the sweetness of the mayflower and the strength of the young oak, but one could easily divine that she was one of 'The souls by nature pitched too high, By suffering plunged too low.'

"That's just the way you look, for all the world as if you did have a lamp burning inside of you," sighed aunt Jane. "Rebecca! I wish you could take things easier, child – I am fearful for you sometimes."

The Robin who Showed the Way

From *The Secret Garden*
by Frances Hodgson Burnett

I have said before, she was not a child who had been trained to ask permission or consult her elders about things. All she thought about the key was that if it was the key to the closed garden, and she could find out where the door was, she could perhaps open it and see what was inside, and what had happened to the old rose-trees. It was because it had been shut up so long that she wanted to see it. Besides that, if she liked it she could go into it every day and shut the door behind her, and could make up some play of her own and play it alone, because nobody would know where she was, but would think the door was still locked and the key buried in the earth. The thought pleased her very much.

Living as it were, all by herself in a house with a hundred mysteriously closed rooms and having nothing whatever to do to amuse herself, had set her inactive brain to working and was actually awakening her imagination. There is no doubt that the fresh, strong, pure air from the moor had a great deal to do with it. In India she had always been too hot and languid and weak to care much about anything, but in this place she was beginning to care and to want to do new things. Already she felt less 'contrary', though she did not know why.

She put the key in her pocket and walked up and down her walk. No one but herself ever seemed to

come there, so she could walk
slowly and look at the wall, or
rather, at the ivy growing on it.
The ivy was the baffling thing.
However carefully she looked
she could see nothing but thickly
growing, glossy, dark green leaves.
She was very disappointed.
Something of her contrariness
came back to her as she paced the
walk and looked over it at the tree-
tops inside. It seemed so silly, she
said to herself, to be near it and not
be able to get in. She took the key
in her pocket when she went back to the house, and
she made up her mind that she would always carry
it with her when she went out, so that if she ever
should find the hidden door she would be ready.

Mrs Medlock had allowed Martha to sleep all
night at the cottage, but she was back at her work in

the morning with cheeks redder than ever and in the best of spirits.

"I got up at four o'clock," she said. "Eh! it was pretty on th' moor with th' birds gettin' up an' th' rabbits scamperin' about an' th' sun risin'. I didn't walk all th' way. A man gave me a ride in his cart an' I did enjoy myself."

She was full of stories of the delights of her day out. Her mother had been glad to see her and they had got all the baking and washing done. She had even made each of the children a doughcake with a bit of brown sugar in it.

"I had 'em all pipin' hot when they came in from playin' on th' moor. An' th' cottage all smelt o' nice, clean hot bakin' an' there was a good fire, an' they just shouted for joy. Our Dickon he said our cottage was good enough for a king."

In the evening they had all sat round the fire, and Martha and her mother had sewed patches on torn clothes and mended stockings and Martha had told them about the little girl who had come from India and who had been waited on all her life until she didn't know how to put on her own stockings.

"Eh! they did like to hear about you," said Martha. "They wanted to know all about th' people you knew an' about th' ship you came in. I couldn't tell 'em enough."

Mary reflected a little. "I'll tell you a great deal more before your next day out," she said, "so that you will have more to talk about. I dare say they would like to hear about riding on elephants and camels, and about the officers going to hunt tigers."

"My word!" cried delighted Martha. "It would set 'em off their heads. It would be same as a wild beast show like we heard they had in York once."

"India is quite different from Yorkshire," Mary said slowly, as she thought the matter over. "I never thought of that. Did Dickon and your mother like to hear you talk about me?"

"Why, our Dickon's eyes nearly started out o' his

head," answered Martha. "But mother, she was put out about your seemin' to be all by yourself like. She said, 'Hasn't Mr Craven got no governess for her?' and I said, 'No, he hasn't, though Mrs Medlock says he will when he thinks of it, but he mayn't think of it for two or three years.'"

"I don't want a governess," said Mary sharply.

"But mother says you ought to be learnin' by this time an' you ought to have a woman to look after you, an' she says: 'Now, Martha, think how you'd feel yourself, in a big place like that, wanderin' about all alone, an' no mother. You do your best to cheer her up,' she says, an' I said I would."

Mary gave her a long, steady look. "You do cheer me up," she said. "I like to hear you talk."

Presently Martha went out of the room and came back with something held in her hands under her apron. "What does tha' think," she said, with a cheerful grin. "I've brought thee a present."

"A present!" exclaimed Mistress Mary. How

could a cottage full of fourteen hungry people give anyone a present?

"A man was drivin' across the moor peddlin'," Martha explained. "An' he stopped his cart at our door. He had pots an' pans an' odds an' ends, but mother had no money to buy anythin'. Just as he was goin' away our 'Lizabeth Ellen called out, 'Mother, he's got skippin'-ropes with red an' blue handles.' An' mother she calls out quite sudden, 'Here, stop, mister! How much are they?' An' he says 'Tuppence', an' mother she began fumblin' in her pocket an' she says to me, 'Martha, tha's brought me thy wages like a good lass, an' I've got four places to put every penny, but I'm just goin' to take tuppence out of it to buy that child a skippin'-rope,' an' she bought one an' here it is."

She brought it out from under her apron and exhibited it quite proudly. It was a strong, slender rope with a striped red and blue handle at each end, but Mary Lennox had never seen a skipping-rope before. She gazed at it with a mystified expression.

"What is it for?" she asked curiously.

"For!" cried out Martha. "Does tha' mean that they've not got skippin'-ropes in India, for all they've got elephants and tigers and camels! This is what it's for; just watch me."

And she ran into the middle of the room and, taking a handle in each hand, began to skip, while Mary turned in her chair to stare at her, and the queer faces in the old portraits seemed to stare at her too, and wonder what on earth this common little cottager had the impudence to be doing under their very noses. But Martha did not even see them. The interest and curiosity in Mistress Mary's face delighted her, and she went on skipping and counted out loud as she skipped until she had reached a hundred.

"I could skip longer than that," she said when she stopped. "I've skipped as much as five hundred in one go when I was twelve, but I wasn't as fat then as I am now, an' I was in practice."

Mary got up from her chair beginning to feel excited herself. "It looks nice," she said. "Your mother is a kind woman. Do you think I could ever skip like that?"

"You just try it," urged Martha, handing her the skipping- rope. "You can't skip a hundred at first, but if you practice you'll mount up. Mother she says, 'Nothin' will do her more good than skippin' rope. It's th' sensiblest toy a child can have. Let her play out in th' fresh air skippin' an' it'll stretch her legs an' arms an' give her some strength in 'em.'"

It was plain that there was not a great deal of strength in Mistress Mary's arms and legs when she first began to skip. She was not very clever at it, but she liked it so much that she did not want to stop.

"Put on tha' things and run an' skip out o' doors," said Martha. "Mother said I must tell you to keep out o' doors as much as you could, even when it rains a bit, so as tha' wrap up warm."

Mary put on her coat and hat and took her skipping-rope over her arm. She opened the door to go out, and then suddenly thought of something and turned back rather slowly.

"Martha," she said, "they were your wages. It was your two-pence really. Thank you." She said it stiffly because she was not used to thanking people or noticing that they did things for her. "Thank you," she said, and held out her hand because she did not know what else to do.

Martha gave her hand a clumsy little shake, as if she was not accustomed to this sort of thing either. Then she laughed. "Run off an' play with thy rope."

Mistress Mary felt a little awkward as she went out of the room.

Yorkshire people seemed strange, and Martha was always rather a puzzle to her. At first she had disliked her very much, but now she did not.

The skipping-rope was a wonderful thing. She counted and skipped, and skipped and counted, until her cheeks were quite red, and she was more interested than she had ever been since she was born. The sun was shining and a little wind was blowing – not a rough wind, but one which came in delightful little gusts and brought a fresh scent of newly turned earth with it.

She skipped round the fountain garden, and up one walk and down another. She skipped at last into the kitchen-garden and saw Ben Weatherstaff digging and talking to his robin, which was hopping about him. She skipped down the walk toward him and he lifted his head and looked at her with a curious expression. She had wondered if he would notice her. She wanted him to see her skip.

"Well!" he exclaimed. "Upon my word. P'raps

tha' art a young 'un, after all, an' p'raps tha's got child's blood in thy veins instead of sour buttermilk. Tha's skipped red into thy cheeks. I wouldn't have believed tha' could do it."

"I never skipped before," Mary said. "I'm just beginning. I can only go up to twenty."

"Tha' keep on," said Ben. "Just see how he's watchin' thee," jerking his head toward the robin. "He followed after thee yesterday. He'll be at it again today. He'll be bound to find out what th' skippin'-rope is. He's never seen one."

Mary skipped round all the gardens and round the orchard, resting every few minutes. At length she went to her own special walk and made up her mind to see if she could skip the whole length of it. It was a good long skip and she began slowly, but before she had gone half-way down the path she was so hot and breathless that she was obliged to stop. She did not mind much, because she had already counted up to thirty. She stopped with a little laugh of pleasure, and there, lo and behold, was the robin swaying on a long branch of ivy. He had followed her and he greeted her with a chirp. As Mary had skipped her way along she had felt something heavy in her pocket strike against her at each jump, and now that she saw the robin she laughed again.

"You showed me where the key was yesterday," she said. "You ought to show me the door today, but I don't believe you know!"

The robin flew from his swinging spray of ivy on to the top of the wall and he opened his beak and sang a loud, lovely trill, merely to show off. Nothing in the world is quite as adorably lovely as a robin when he shows off – and they are nearly always doing it.

Mary Lennox had heard a great deal about magic in her Ayah's stories, and she always said that what happened almost at that moment was magic. One of the nice little gusts of wind rushed down the

walk, and it was a stronger one than the rest. It was
strong enough to wave the branches of the trees,
and it was more than strong enough to sway the
trailing sprays of untrimmed ivy hanging from the
wall. Mary had stepped close to the robin, and
suddenly the gust of wind swung aside some loose
ivy trails, and more suddenly still she jumped
toward it and caught it in her hand. This she did
because she had seen something under it – a round
knob that had been covered by the leaves hanging
over it. It was the knob of a door.

She put her hands under the leaves and began to
pull and push them aside. Thick as the ivy hung, it
nearly all was a loose and swinging curtain, though
some had crept over wood and iron. Mary's heart
began to thump and her hands to shake a little in
her delight and excitement. The robin kept singing
and twittering away and tilting his head on one
side, as if he were as excited as she was. What was
this under her hands which was square and made of

iron and which her fingers found a hole in?

It was the lock of the door that had been closed ten years and she put her hand in her pocket, drew out the key and found it fitted the keyhole. She put the key in and turned it. It took two hands to do it, but it did turn. And then she took a long breath and looked behind her up the long walk to see if anyone was coming. No one ever did come, it seemed, and she took another long breath, because she could not help it, and she held back the swinging curtain of ivy and pushed back the door that opened slowly.

Then she slipped through it, and shut it behind her, and stood with her back against it, looking about her and breathing quite fast with excitement, and wonder, and delight.

She was standing inside the secret garden.

SAVING THE DAY

A Stormy Day

From *Black Beauty*
by Anna Sewell

One day late in the autumn my master had a long journey to go on business. I was put into the dog-cart, and John went with his master. I always liked to go in the dog-cart, it was so light and the high wheels ran along so pleasantly. There had been a great deal of rain, and now the wind was very high and blew the dry leaves across the road in a shower. We went along merrily till we came to the toll-bar and the low wooden bridge. The river banks were rather high, and the bridge, instead of rising, went across just level, so that in the middle, if the river was full, the water would be nearly up to the woodwork, but as there were good substantial rails on each side, people did not mind it.

The man at the gate said the river was rising fast, and he feared it would be a bad night. In one low part of the road the water was halfway up to my knees. The bottom was good, and master drove gently, so it was no matter.

When we got to the town of course I had a good bait, but as the master's business engaged him a long time we did not start for home till late in the afternoon. The wind was then much higher, and I heard the master say to John that he had never been out in such a storm. And so I thought, as we went along the skirts of a wood, where the great branches were swaying about like twigs, and the rushing sound was terrible.

"I wish we were well out of this wood," said my master in a low voice.

"Yes, sir," said John, "it would be rather awkward if one of these branches came down upon us."

The words were scarcely out of his mouth when there was a groan, and a crack, and a splitting sound, and tearing, crashing down among the other trees came an oak, torn up by the roots, and it fell right across the road just before us. I will never say I was not frightened, for I was. I stopped still, and I believe I trembled; of course I did not turn round or run away – I was not brought up to that. John jumped out and was in a moment at my head.

"That was a very near touch," said my master. "What's to be done now?"

"Well, sir, we can't drive over that tree, nor yet get round it. There will be nothing for it, but to go back and that will be a good six miles before we get round to the wooden bridge again."

So back we went and round by the crossroads, but by the time we got to the bridge it was very nearly dark; we could just see that the water was

A Stormy Day

over the middle of it; but as that happened sometimes when the floods were out, master did not stop. We were going along at a good pace, but the moment my feet touched the first part of the bridge I felt sure there was something wrong. I dare not go forward, and I made a dead stop. "Go on,

Beauty," said my master, and he gave me a touch
with the whip, but I dare not stir. He gave me a
sharp cut; I jumped, but I dare not go forward.

"There's something wrong, sir," said John, and he
sprang out of the dog-cart and came to my head and
looked all about. He tried to lead me forward.
"Come on, Beauty, what's the matter?" Of course I
could not tell him, but I knew very well that the
bridge was not safe.

Just then the man at the toll-gate on the other
side ran out of the house, tossing a torch about like
one mad.

"Hoy, hoy, hoy! Halloo! Stop!" he cried.

"What's the matter?" shouted my master.

"The bridge is broken in the middle, and part of
it has been carried away; if you come on you'll be
into the river."

"Thank God!" said my master.

"You Beauty!" said John, and took the bridle and
gently turned me round. The wind seemed to have

lulled off after that furious blast which tore up the tree. It grew darker and darker, stiller and stiller. I trotted quietly along, the wheels hardly making a sound on the soft road. For a good while neither master nor John spoke, and then master began in a serious voice. I could not understand much of what they said, but I found they thought, if I had gone on as the master wanted me, most likely the bridge would have given way under us, and horse, chaise, master, and man would have fallen into the river; and as the current was flowing very strongly, it was more than likely we should all have been drowned. Master said, "God had given men reason by which they could find out things for themselves; but he had given animals knowledge that did not depend on reason, and which was much more prompt and perfect in its way, and by which they had often saved the lives of men." John thought people did not value their animals half enough nor make friends of them as they ought to do.

SAVING THE DAY

At last we came to the park gates and found the gardener looking out for us. He said that mistress had been in a dreadful way ever since dark, fearing some accident had happened, and that she had sent James off on Justice, the roan cob, toward the bridge to enquire after us. As we approached, mistress ran out, saying,

"Have you had an accident?"

"No, my dear; but if your Black Beauty had not been wiser than we were we should all have been carried down the river at the wooden bridge."

Oh, what a good supper he gave me that night – a good bran mash and some crushed beans with my oats, and such a thick bed of straw! And I was glad of it, for I was tired.

Christmas Wishes

From *Little Women*
by Louisa May Alcott

The March girls are four sisters. They live with their mother while their father is away from home as Army Chaplain in the Civil War.

Jo lay on the rug and grumbled, "Christmas won't be Christmas without any presents."

"It's so dreadful to be poor!" sighed Meg, looking down at her old dress.

"I don't think it's fair for some girls to have plenty of pretty things, and other girls nothing at all," added little Amy, with an injured sniff.

"We've got Father and Mother, and each other,"
said Beth contentedly from her corner.

The four young faces on which the firelight
shone brightened at the cheerful words, but
darkened again as Jo said sadly, "We haven't got
Father, and shall not have him for a long time." She

didn't say perhaps never, but each silently added it, thinking of Father far away, where the fighting was.

Nobody spoke for a minute; then Meg said, "You know the reason Mother proposed not having any presents this Christmas was because it is going to be a hard winter for everyone; and she thinks we ought not to spend money for pleasure, when our men are suffering so in the army. We can't do much, but we can make our little sacrifices, and ought to do it gladly. But I am afraid I don't." And Meg shook her head, as she thought regretfully of all the pretty things she wanted.

"But I don't think the little we should spend would do any good. We've each got a dollar, and the army wouldn't be much helped by our giving that. I agree not to expect anything from Mother or you, but I do want to buy *Undine* and *Sintram* for myself. I've wanted it so long", said Jo, who was a bookworm.

"I planned to spend mine in new music," said

Beth, with a little sigh, which no one heard but the hearth brush and kettle holder.

"I shall get a nice box of Faber's drawing pencils. I really need them," said Amy decidedly.

"Mother didn't say anything to us about our money, and she won't wish us to give up everything. Let's each buy something we want, and have a little fun. I'm sure we all work hard enough to earn it," cried Jo, examining the heels of her shoes in a gentlemanly manner.

"I know I do – teaching those tiresome children nearly all day, when I'm longing to enjoy myself at home," began Meg, in the complaining tone again.

"You don't have half such a hard time as I do," said Jo. "How would you like to be shut up for hours with great-aunt March – such a nervous, fussy old lady, who keeps you trotting, is never satisfied, and worries you till you're just about ready to fly out of the window or cry?"

"It's naughty to fret, but I do think washing

dishes and keeping things tidy is the worst work in the world. My hands get so stiff, I can't practice well." And Beth looked at her rough hands with a sigh that anyone could hear that time.

"I don't believe any of you suffer as I do," cried Amy. "For you don't have to go to school with impertinent girls, who plague you if you don't know your lessons, and laugh at your dresses, and label your father if he isn't rich, and insult you when your nose isn't nice."

"If you mean libel, you should say so, and not talk about labels, as if Papa was a pickle bottle," advised Jo, laughing.

"I know what I mean, and you needn't be satirical about it. It's proper to try to use good words, and improve your vocabulary," returned Amy, with dignity.

"Don't peck at one another, children. Don't you wish we had the money Papa lost when we were little, Jo? Dear me! How happy and good we'd be, if we had no worries!" said Meg, who could remember better times.

"You said the other day you thought we were a deal happier than the King children, for they were fighting and fretting all the time, in spite of all their money."

"So I did, Beth. Well, I think we are. For though we do have to work, we make fun of ourselves, and are a pretty jolly set, as Jo would say."

"Jo does use such slang words!" observed Amy, with a reproving look at the long figure stretched on the rug.

Jo immediately sat up, put her hands in her pockets, and began to whistle.

"Don't, Jo. It's so boyish!"

"That's why I do it."

"I detest rude, unladylike girls!"

"I hate affected, niminy-piminy chits!"

"Birds in their little nests agree," sang Beth, the peacemaker, with such a funny face that both sharp voices softened to a laugh, and the pecking ended for that time.

"Really, girls, you are both to be blamed," said Meg, beginning to lecture in her elder-sisterly fashion. "You are old enough to leave off boyish tricks, and to behave better, Josephine. It didn't matter so much when you were a little girl, but now you are so tall, and turn up your hair, you should remember that you are a young lady."

"I'm not! And if turning up my hair makes me one, I'll wear it in two tails till I'm twenty," cried Jo. "I hate to think I've got to grow up, and be Miss March, and wear long gowns, and look as prim as a China Aster! It's bad enough to be a girl, anyway, when I like boy's games and work and manners! I can't get over my disappointment in not being a boy. And it's worse than ever now, for I'm dying to go and fight with Papa. And I can only stay home and knit, like a poky old woman!"

And Jo shook the blue army sock till the needles

rattled like castanets, and her ball bounded across the room.

"Poor Jo! It's too bad, but it can't be helped. So you must try to be contented with making your name boyish, and playing brother to us girls," said Beth, stroking the rough head with a hand that all the dish washing and dusting in the world could not make ungentle in its touch.

"As for you, Amy," continued Meg, "you are altogether too particular and prim. Your airs are funny now, but you'll grow up an affected little goose, if you don't take care. I like your nice manners and refined ways of speaking, when you don't try to be elegant. But your absurd words are as bad as Jo's slang."

Christmas Wishes

"If Jo is a tomboy and Amy a goose, what am I, please?" asked Beth, ready to share the lecture.

"You're a dear, and nothing else", answered Meg warmly, and no one contradicted her, for the 'Mouse' was the pet of the family.

As young readers like to know 'how people look', we will take this moment to give them a little sketch of the four sisters, who sat knitting away in the twilight, while the December snow fell quietly without, and the fire crackled cheerfully within. It was a comfortable room, though the carpet was faded and the furniture very plain, for a good picture or two hung on the walls, books filled the recesses, chrysanthemums and Christmas roses bloomed in the windows, and a pleasant atmosphere of home peace pervaded it.

Margaret, the eldest of the four, was sixteen, and very pretty, with large eyes, plenty of soft fair hair, a sweet mouth, and white hands, of which she was rather vain.

Fifteen-year-old Jo was very tall, thin, and brown, and reminded one of a colt, for she never seemed to know what to do with her long limbs, which were very much in her way. She had a decided mouth, a comical nose, and sharp, grey eyes, which appeared to see everything, and were by turns fierce, funny, or thoughtful. Her long, thick hair was her one beauty, but it was usually bundled into a net, to be out of her way. Round shoulders had Jo, big hands and feet, a fly-away look to her clothes, and the uncomfortable appearance of a girl who was rapidly shooting up into a woman and didn't like it.

Elizabeth, or Beth, as everyone called her, was a rosy, smooth-haired, bright-eyed girl of thirteen, with a shy manner, a soft, timid voice, and a peaceful expression which was seldom disturbed. Her father often called her 'Miss Tranquillity', and the name suited her excellently, for she seemed to live in a happy little world of her own, only venturing out to meet the few whom she trusted and loved.

Amy, though the youngest, was a most important person, in her own opinion at least. A regular snow maiden, with blue eyes, and yellow hair curling on her shoulders, pale and slender, and always carrying herself like a young lady mindful of her manners. What the characters of the four sisters were we will leave to be found out.

The clock struck six and, having swept up the hearth, Beth put a pair of slippers down to warm. Somehow the sight of the old shoes had a good effect upon the girls, for Mother was coming, and everyone brightened to welcome her. Meg stopped lecturing, and lighted the lamp, Amy drew the easy chair into the best position by the fire, and Jo forgot how tired she was as she sat up to hold the slippers nearer to the blaze.

"They are quite worn out. Marmee must have a new pair."

"I thought I'd get her some with my dollar," said Beth.

"No, I shall!" cried Amy.

"I'm the oldest," began Meg, but Jo cut in with a decided, "I'm the man of the family now Papa is away, and I shall provide the slippers, for he told me to take special care of Mother while he was gone."

"I'll tell you what we'll do," said Beth, "let's each get her something for Christmas, and not get anything for ourselves."

"That's like you, dear! What will we get?" exclaimed Jo.

Everyone thought soberly for a minute, then Meg announced, as if the idea was suggested by the sight of her own pretty hands, "I shall give her a nice pair of gloves."

Christmas Wishes

"Army shoes, best to be had," cried Jo.

"Some handkerchiefs, all hemmed," said Beth.

"I'll get a little bottle of cologne. She likes it, and it won't cost much, so I'll have some left to buy my pencils," added Amy.

"How will we give the things?" asked Meg.

"Put them on the table, and bring her in and see her open the bundles. Don't you remember how we used to do on our birthdays?" answered Jo.

"I used to be so frightened when it was my turn to sit in the chair with the crown on, and see you all come marching round to give the presents, with a kiss. I liked the things and the kisses, but it was dreadful to have you sit looking at me while I opened the bundles," said Beth, who was toasting her face and the bread for tea at the same time.

"Let Marmee think we are getting things for ourselves, and then surprise her. We must go shopping tomorrow afternoon, Meg. There is so much to do about the play for Christmas night," said Jo, marching up and down, with her hands behind her back, and her nose in the air.

"I don't mean to act any more after this time. I'm getting too old for such things," observed Meg.

"You won't stop, I know, as long as you can trail round in a white gown with your hair down, and wear gold-paper jewellery. You are the best actress we've got, and there'll be an end of everything if you quit the boards," said Jo. "We ought to rehearse tonight. Come here, Amy, and do the fainting scene, for you are as stiff as a poker in that."

"I can't help it. I never saw anyone faint, and I don't choose to make myself all black and blue, tumbling flat as you do. If I can go down easily, I'll drop. If I can't, I shall fall into a chair and be graceful. I don't care if Hugo does come at me with a pistol," returned Amy, who was not gifted with dramatic power, but was chosen because she was small enough to be borne out shrieking by the villain of the piece.

"Do it this way. Clasp your hands so, and stagger across the room, crying frantically, 'Roderigo Save me! Save me!'" and away went Jo, with a melodramatic scream that was truly thrilling.

Amy followed, but she poked her hands out stiffly before her, and jerked herself along as if she went by machinery, and her "Ow!" was more suggestive of pins being run into her than of fear and anguish. Jo gave a despairing groan, and Meg laughed outright, while Beth let her bread burn as she watched the fun with interest.

"It's no use! Do the best you can when the time comes, and if the audience laughs, don't blame me. Come on, Meg."

Then things went smoothly, for Don Pedro defied the world in a speech of two pages without a single break. Hagar, the witch, chanted an awful incantation over her kettleful of simmering toads, with weird effect. Roderigo rent his chains asunder manfully, and Hugo died in agonies of remorse and arsenic, with a wild, "Ha! Ha!"

"It's the best we've had yet", said Meg, as the dead villain sat up and rubbed his elbows.

"I don't see how you can write and act such splendid things, Jo. You're a regular Shakespeare!" exclaimed Beth, who firmly believed that her sisters were gifted with wonderful genius in all things.

"Not quite," replied Jo modestly. "I do think *The Witches Curse, an Operatic Tragedy* is rather a nice thing, but I'd like to try *MacBeth*, if we only had a trapdoor for Banquo. I always wanted to do the killing part. 'Is that a dagger that I see before me?'" muttered Jo, rolling her eyes and clutching at the air, as she had seen a famous tragedian do.

"No, it's the toasting fork, with Mother's shoe on it instead of the bread. Beth's stage-struck!" cried Meg, and the rehearsal ended in a burst of laughter.

"Glad to find you so merry, my girls," said a cheery voice at the door, and actors and audience turned to welcome a tall, motherly lady with a 'can I

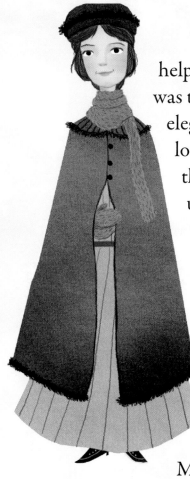

help you' look about her which was truly delightful. She was not elegantly dressed, but a noble-looking woman, and the girls thought the plain cloak and unfashionable bonnet covered the most splendid mother in the world.

"Well, dearies, how have you got on today? There was so much to do, getting the boxes ready to go tomorrow, that I didn't come home to dinner. Has anyone called, Beth? How is your cold, Meg? Jo, you look tired to death. Come and kiss me, baby."

While making these maternal inquiries Mrs March got her wet things off, her warm slippers on, and sitting down in the easy chair, drew

Amy to her lap, preparing to enjoy the happiest hour of her busy day. The girls flew about, trying to make things comfortable. Meg arranged the tea table, Jo brought wood and set chairs, dropping, over-turning, and clattering everything she touched. Beth trotted to and fro between parlour and kitchen, quiet and busy, while Amy gave directions to everyone, as she sat with her hands folded.

As they gathered about the table, Mrs March said, with a particularly happy face, "I've got a treat for you after supper."

A quick, bright smile went round like a streak of sunshine. Beth clapped her hands, regardless of the biscuit she held, and Jo tossed up her napkin, crying, "A letter! A letter! Three cheers for Father!"

"Yes, a nice long letter. He is well, and thinks he shall get through the cold season better than we feared. He sends loving wishes for Christmas, and an especial message to you girls," said Mrs March, patting her pocket as if she had got a treasure there.

Christmas Wishes

"Hurry and get done! Don't stop to quirk your little finger and simper over your plate, Amy," cried Jo, choking on her tea and dropping her bread, butter side down, on the carpet in her haste to get at the treat.

Beth ate no more, but crept away to sit in her shadowy corner and brood over the delight to come, till the others were ready.

"I think it was so splendid in Father to go as chaplain when he was too old to be drafted, and not strong enough for a soldier," said Meg warmly.

"Don't I wish I could go as a drummer, a vivan – what's its name? Or a nurse, so I could be near him and help him," exclaimed Jo, with a groan.

"It must be very disagreeable to sleep in a tent, and eat all sorts of bad-tasting things, and drink out of a tin mug," sighed Amy.

"When will he come home, Marmee?" asked Beth, with a little quiver in her voice.

"Not for many months, dear, unless he is sick.

He will do his work faithfully as long as he can, and we won't ask for him back a minute sooner than he can be spared. Now come and hear the letter."

They all drew to the fire, Mother in the big chair with Beth at her feet, Meg and Amy perched on either arm of the chair, and Jo leaning on the back, where no one would see any emotion if the letter should happen to be touching. Very few letters were written in those hard times that were not touching, especially those that fathers sent home. In this one little was said of the hardships endured, the dangers faced, or the homesickness conquered.

It was a cheerful, hopeful letter, full of lively descriptions of camp life, marches, and military news, and only at the end did the writer's heart overflow with fatherly love and longing for the little girls at home:

Give them all of my dear love and a kiss. Tell them I think of them by day, pray for them by night, and find my best comfort in their affection always. A year

seems a very long time to wait before I can see them again, but remind them that while we wait we may all work, so that these hard days need not be wasted. I know they will remember all that I said to them, that they will be loving children to you, will do their duty faithfully, and conquer themselves so beautifully that when I come back to them I may be fonder and prouder than ever of my little women.

Everybody sniffed when they came to that part. Jo wasn't ashamed of the great tear that dropped off the end of her nose, and Amy hid her face on her mother's shoulder and sobbed, "I am a selfish girl! But I'll truly try to be better, so he mayn't be disappointed in me by-and-by."

"We all will," cried Meg. "I think too much of my looks and hate to work, but won't any more, if I can help it."

"I'll try hard to be what he loves to call me, 'a little woman' and not be rough and wild, and I shall try to do my duty here instead of wanting to be somewhere else," said Jo, thinking that keeping her temper at home was a much harder task than facing a rebel or two down South.

Beth said nothing, but quietly wiped away her tears with one of the blue army socks and began to knit at once with all her might, losing no time in doing the duty that lay nearest her, while she resolved in her quiet little soul to be all that Father hoped to find her when the year brought round the happy coming home.

Mrs March broke the silence that followed Jo's words, by saying, "Do you remember how you used to play Pilgrims' Progress when you were little? Nothing delighted you more than to tie my piece bags on your backs for burdens, give you sticks and rolls of paper, and let you travel through the house from the cellar, which was the City of Destruction, to the housetop, where you had lovely things you could collect to make a Celestial City."

"I liked the place where the bundles fell off and tumbled downstairs," said Meg.

"I don't remember much about it, except that I was afraid of the cellar, and always liked the cake and milk we had up at the top. If I wasn't too old for such things, I'd rather like to play it over again," said Amy, who began to talk of renouncing childish things at the mature age of twelve.

"We never are too old for this, my dear, because it is a play we are playing all the time in one way or another. Our burdens are here, our road is before us, and the longing for goodness and happiness is the guide that leads us through many troubles and mistakes to the peace which is a true Celestial City. Now, my little pilgrims, suppose you begin again, not in play, but in earnest, and see how far on you can get before Father comes home."

"Really, Mother? Where are our bundles?" asked Amy, who was a very literal young lady.

"Each of you told what your burden was just

now, except Beth. I rather think she hasn't got any," said her mother.

"I have. Mine is dishes and dusters, and envying girls with nice pianos, and being afraid of people."

Beth's bundle was so funny that everybody wanted to laugh, but nobody did, for it would have hurt her feelings very much.

"Let us do it," said Meg thoughtfully. It is only another name for trying to be good, and the story may help us."

Then out came the four work baskets, and the needles flew as the girls made sheets for Aunt March. It was uninteresting sewing, but tonight no one grumbled. They adopted Jo's plan of dividing the long seams into four parts, and calling the quarters Europe, Asia, Africa, and America, and in that way got on capitally, especially when they talked about the different countries as they stitched their way through them.

At nine they stopped work, and sang, before

they went to bed. No one but Beth could get much music out of the old piano, but she had a way of softly touching the yellow keys and making a pleasant accompaniment to the simple songs they sang. Meg had a voice like a flute, and she and her mother led the little choir. Amy chirped like a cricket, and Jo wandered through the airs at her own sweet will, always coming out at the wrong place with a croak or a quaver that spoiled the most pensive tune. They had done this from the time they could lisp 'Crinkle, crinkle, 'ittle 'tar', and it had become a household custom, for mother was a born singer. The first sound in the morning was her voice as she went about the house singing like a lark, and the last sound at night was the same cheery sound, for the girls never grew too old for that familiar lullaby.

The Wild Wood

From *The Wind in the Willows*
by Kenneth Grahame

The Mole wanted to make the acquaintance of the Badger. He seemed, by all accounts, to be such an important personage and, though rarely visible, to make his unseen influence felt by everybody about the place. But whenever the Mole mentioned his wish to the Water Rat he always found himself put off. "It's all right," the Rat would say. "Badger'll turn up some day or other – he's always turning up – and then I'll introduce you. The best of fellows! But you must not only take him as you find him, but when you find him."

"Couldn't you ask him here to dinner or something?" said the Mole.

"He wouldn't come," replied the Rat simply. "Badger hates Society, and invitations, and dinner, and all that sort of thing."

"Well, then, supposing we go and call on him?" suggested the Mole.

"Oh, I'm sure he wouldn't like that at all," said the Rat, quite alarmed. "He's so very shy, he'd be sure to be offended. I've never even ventured to call on him at his own home myself, though I know him so well. Besides, we can't. It's quite out of the question, because he lives in the very middle of the Wild Wood."

"Well, supposing he does," said the Mole. "You told me the Wild Wood was all right, you know."

"Oh, I know, I know, so it is," replied the Rat evasively. "But I think we won't go there just now. Not just yet. It's a long way, and he wouldn't be at

The Wild Wood

home at this time of year anyhow, and he'll be coming along some day, if you'll wait quietly."

The Mole had to be content with this. But the Badger never came along, and it was not till summer was long over, and cold and frost kept them much indoors, and the swollen river raced past outside their windows with a speed that mocked at boating of any sort or kind, that he found his thoughts dwelling again on the solitary grey Badger, who lived his own life by himself, in his hole in the middle of the Wild Wood.

In the winter time the Rat slept a great deal, retiring early and rising late. During his short day he sometimes scribbled poetry or did small jobs about the house; and, of course, there were always a stream of animals dropping in for a chat, and consequently a good deal of story-telling and comparing notes on the past summer and all its doings.

There was plenty to talk about on those short winter days when the animals found themselves round the fire; still, the Mole had a good deal of spare time on his hands, and so one afternoon, when the Rat in his armchair before the blaze was alternately dozing and trying over rhymes that wouldn't fit, he formed the resolution to go out by himself and explore the Wild Wood, and perhaps strike up an acquaintance with Mr Badger.

It was a cold, still afternoon with a hard steely sky overhead, when he slipped out of the warm parlour into the open air. The country lay bare and entirely leafless around him, and he thought that he had never seen so far and so intimately into the insides of things as on that winter day when Nature was deep in her annual slumber and seemed to have kicked the clothes off.

The Wild Wood

Copses, dells, quarries and all hidden places, which had been mysterious mines for exploration in leafy summer, now exposed themselves and their secrets pathetically, and seemed to ask him to overlook their shabby poverty for a while, till they could riot in rich masquerade as before, and trick and entice him with the old deceptions. It was pitiful in a way, and yet cheering. He was glad that he liked the country undecorated, and stripped of its finery. He had got down to the bare bones of it, and they were fine and strong and simple. He did not want the warm clover and the play of seeding grasses; the billowy drapery of beech and elm seemed best away; and with great cheerfulness of spirit he pushed on towards the Wild Wood, which lay before him low and threatening, like a black reef in some still southern sea.

There was nothing to alarm him at first entry. Twigs crackled under his feet, logs tripped him, funguses on stumps resembled caricatures, and

startled him for the moment by their likeness to
something familiar and far away; but that was all
fun, and exciting. It led him on, and he penetrated
to where the light was less, and trees crouched
nearer and nearer, and holes made ugly mouths at
him on either side.

Everything was very still now. The dusk
advanced on him steadily, rapidly, gathering in
behind and before; and the light seemed to be
draining away like flood-water.

Then the faces began.

It was over his shoulder, and indistinctly, that he
first thought he saw a face, a tiny evil wedge-shaped
face, looking out at him from a hole. But when he
turned and confronted it, the thing had vanished.

He quickened his pace, telling himself cheerfully
not to begin imagining things, or there would be
simply no end to it. He passed another hole, and
another, and another; and then – yes! – no! – yes!
certainly a little narrow face, with hard eyes, had

flashed up for an instant from a hole, and was gone. He hesitated – braced himself up for an effort and strode on. Then suddenly, and as if it had been so all the time, every hole, far and near – and there were hundreds of them – seemed to possess its own face, coming and going rapidly, all fixing on him glances of malice and hatred: all hard-eyed and evil and sharp.

If he could only get away from the holes in the banks, he thought, there would be no more faces. He swung off the path and plunged into the untrodden places of the wood.

Then the whistling began.

Very faint and shrill it was, and far behind him, when first he heard it; but somehow it made him hurry forward. Then, still very faint and shrill, it sounded far ahead of him, and made him hesitate and want to go back. As he halted in indecision it broke out on either side, and seemed to be caught up and passed on throughout the whole length of

the wood to its farthest limit. They were up and
alert and ready, evidently, whoever they were!
And he – he was alone, and unarmed, and far from
any help; and the night was closing in.

Then the pattering began.
He thought it was only falling leaves at first, so
slight and delicate was the sound of it. Then as it

grew it took a regular rhythm, and he knew it for nothing else but the pat-pat-pat of little feet still a very long way off. Was it in front or behind? It seemed to be first one, and then the other, then both. It grew and it multiplied, till from every quarter as he listened anxiously, leaning this way and that, it seemed to be closing in on him. As he stood still to hearken, a rabbit came running hard towards him through the trees. He waited, expecting it to slacken pace, or to swerve from him into a different course. It stopped and looked at him, before dashing onwards. "Get out of this, you fool, get out!" the Mole heard him mutter as he swung round a stump and disappeared down a friendly burrow.

The pattering increased till it sounded like sudden hail on the dry leaf-carpet spread around him. The whole wood seemed running now, running hard, hunting, chasing, closing in round something or – somebody? In panic, he began to run too, aimlessly, he knew not whither. He ran up against things, he fell over things and into things, he darted under things and dodged round things.

At last he took refuge in the deep dark hollow of an old beech tree, which offered shelter and concealment – and perhaps even safety, but who could be sure? Anyhow, he was too exhausted to run any further, and could only snuggle down into the dry leaves that had drifted into the hollow and hope he was safe for a time. And as the Mole lay in the dark, panting and trembling, and listened to the whistlings and hootings and patterings outside, he knew it at last, in all its fullness: that dread thing, which other little dwellers in field and hedgerow had encountered here, and known as their darkest moment. It was the thing which the kind Rat had tried in vain to shield him from – the Terror of the Wild Wood!

Meantime the Rat, warm and comfortable, dozed by his fireside. His paper of half-finished

verses slipped from his knee, his head fell back, his mouth opened, and he wandered by the verdant banks of dream-rivers. Then a coal slipped, the fire crackled and sent up a spurt of flame, and he woke with a start. Remembering what he had been engaged upon, he reached down to the floor for his verses, pored over them for a minute, and then looked round for the Mole to ask him if he knew a good rhyme for something or other.

But the Mole was not there.

The Rat listened for a time. The house seemed very quiet.

Then he called "Moly!" several times. Receiving no answer, he got up and went out into the hall.

The Mole's cap was missing from its accustomed peg. His goloshes, which always lay by the umbrella-stand, were also gone.

The Rat left the house, and carefully examined the muddy surface of the ground outside, hoping to find the Mole's tracks. There they were, sure enough. The goloshes were new, just bought for the winter, and the pimples on their soles were fresh and sharp. He could see the imprints of them in the mud, running along straight and purposeful, leading direct to the Wild Wood.

The Rat looked very grave, and stood in deep thought for a minute or two. Then he re-entered the house, strapped a belt round his waist, shoved a brace of pistols into it, took up a stout cudgel that stood in a corner of the hall, and set off for the Wild Wood at a smart pace.

It was already getting towards dusk when he reached the first fringe of trees and plunged without hesitation into the wood, looking anxiously on either side for any sign of his friend. Here and there wicked little faces popped out of holes, but vanished immediately at sight of the valorous animal, his pistols, and the great ugly cudgel in his grasp; and the whistling and pattering, which he had heard quite plainly on his first entry, died away

The Wild Wood

and ceased, and all was very still. He made
his way manfully through the length of the
wood, to its furthest edge; then, forsaking
all paths, he set himself to traverse it,
laboriously working over the whole
ground, and all the time calling out
cheerfully, "Moly, Moly, Moly! Where
are you? It's me – it's old Rat!"

He had patiently hunted
through the wood for an hour
or more, when at last to his
joy he heard a little
answering cry. Guiding himself by
the sound, he made his way
through the gathering darkness
to the foot of an old beech tree,
with a hole in it, and from out
of the hole came a feeble voice,
saying, "Ratty! Is that
really you?"

SAVING THE DAY

So the Mole got well into the dry leaves and stretched himself out, and presently dropped off into sleep, though of a broken and troubled sort; while the Rat covered himself up, too, as best he might, for warmth, and lay patiently waiting, with a pistol in his paw.

When at last the Mole woke up, much refreshed and in his usual spirits, the Rat said, "Now then! I'll just take a look outside and see if everything's quiet, and then we really must be off."

He went to the entrance of their retreat and put his head out. Then the Mole heard him saying quietly to himself, "Hullo! hullo! here is a go!"

"What's up, Ratty?" asked the Mole.

"Snow is up," replied the Rat briefly; "or rather, down. It's snowing hard."

The Mole came and crouched beside him, and, looking out, saw the wood that had been so dreadful to him in quite a changed aspect. Holes, hollows, pitfalls, and other black menaces to the wayfarer were vanishing fast, and a gleaming carpet of fairy was springing up everywhere, that looked too delicate to be trodden upon by rough feet. A fine powder filled the air and caressed the cheek with a tingle in its touch, and the trees showed up in a light that seemed to come from below.

"Well, well, it can't be helped," said the Rat, after pondering. "We must make a start, and take our chance, I suppose. The worst of it is, I don't exactly know where we are. And now this snow makes everything look so very different."

It did indeed. The Mole would not have known that it was the same wood. However, they set out bravely, and took the line that seemed most promising, holding on to each other and pretending with cheerfulness that they recognized an old friend in every fresh tree that grimly and silently greeted them, or saw openings, gaps, or paths with a familiar turn in them, in the monotony of white space and black tree trunks that refused to vary.

SAVING THE DAY

An hour or two later they sat down on a fallen tree trunk to recover their breath and consider what was to be done. They were aching with fatigue and bruised with tumbles; they had fallen into several holes and got wet through; and the trees were thicker and more like each other than ever. There seemed to be no end to this wood, and no beginning, and no difference in it, and, worst of all, no way out.

"We can't sit here very long," said the Rat. "We shall have to make another push for it, and do something or other. The cold is too awful for anything, and the snow will soon be too deep for us to wade through." He peered about him and considered. "Look here," he went on, "this is what occurs to me. There's a sort of dell down here in front of us, where the ground seems all hilly and humpy and hummocky. We'll make our way down into that, and try and find some sort of shelter, a cave or hole with a dry floor to it, out of the snow and the wind, and there we'll have a good rest before we try again, for we're both of us pretty dead beat. Besides, the snow may leave off, or something may turn up."

So once more they got on their feet, and struggled down into the dell, where they hunted about for a cave or some corner that was dry and a protection from the keen wind and the whirling snow. They were investigating one of the hummocky bits the Rat had spoken of, when suddenly the Mole tripped up and fell forward on his face with a squeal.

"Oh my leg!" he cried. "Oh my poor shin!" and he sat up on the snow and nursed his leg in both his front paws.

"Poor old Mole!" said the Rat kindly. "You don't seem to be having much luck today, do you? Let's have a look at the leg. Yes," he went on, going down on his knees to look, "you've cut your shin, sure enough. Wait till I get at my handkerchief, and I'll tie it up for you."

"I must have tripped over a hidden branch or a stump," said the Mole miserably. "Oh, my!"

"It's a very clean cut," said the Rat, examining it again attentively. "That was never done by a branch. Looks as if it was made by a sharp edge of metal. Funny!" He pondered awhile, and examined the humps and slopes that surrounded them.

"Well, never mind what done it," said the Mole, forgetting his grammar in his pain. "It hurts just the same, whatever done it."

But the Rat, after carefully tying up the leg with his handkerchief, had left him and was busy scraping in the snow. He scratched and shovelled and explored, while the Mole waited impatiently, remarking at intervals, "Oh, come on, Rat!"

Suddenly the Rat cried "Hooray!" and then "Hooray-oo-ray-oo-ray-oo-ray!" and fell to executing a feeble jig in the snow.

"What have you found, Ratty?" asked the Mole,

still nursing his leg.

"Come and see!" said the delighted Rat, as he jigged on.

The Mole hobbled up to the spot and had a good look.

"Well," he said at last, slowly, "I see it right enough. Seen the same sort of thing before, lots of times. A door-scraper! Well, what of it? Why dance jigs around a door-scraper?"

"But don't you see what it means, you – you dull-witted animal?" cried the Rat impatiently.

"Of course I see what it means," replied the Mole. "It simply means that some very careless and forgetful person has left his door-scraper lying about in the middle of the Wild Wood, just where it's sure to trip everybody up. Very thoughtless of him, I call it. When I get home I shall go and complain about it to – to somebody or other, see if I don't!"

"Oh, dear! Oh, dear!" cried the Rat, in despair at

his obtuseness. "Here, stop arguing and come and scrape!" And he set to work again and made the snow fly in all directions around him.

After some further toil his efforts were rewarded, and a very shabby door mat lay exposed to view.

"There, what did I tell you?" exclaimed the Rat in great triumph.

"Absolutely nothing whatever," replied the Mole, with perfect truthfulness. "Well now," he went on, "you seem to have found another piece of domestic litter, and I suppose you're perfectly happy. Better go ahead and dance your jig round that if you've got to, and get it over, and then perhaps we can go on and not waste any more time over rubbish-heaps. Can we eat a door mat? Or sleep under a door mat? Or sit on a door mat and sledge home over the snow on it, you exasperating rodent?"

"Do you mean to say," cried the excited Rat, "that this door mat doesn't tell you anything?"

"Really, Rat," said the Mole, quite pettishly, "I think we'd had enough of this folly. Who ever heard of a door mat telling anyone anything? They simply don't do it. They are not that sort at all. Door mats know their place."

"Now look here, you – you thick-headed beast," replied the Rat, really angry, "this must stop. Not another word, but scrape and scratch and dig and hunt round, especially on the sides of the hummocks, if you want to sleep dry and warm tonight, for it's our last chance!"

The Rat attacked a snowbank beside them with

ardour, probing with his cudgel everywhere and then digging with fury; and the Mole scraped busily too, more to oblige the Rat than for any other reason, for his opinion was that his friend was getting light-headed.

Some ten minutes' hard work, and the point of the Rat's cudgel struck something that sounded hollow. He worked till he could get a paw through and feel; then called the Mole to come and help him. Hard at it went the two animals, till at last the result of their labours stood full in view of the astonished and hitherto incredulous Mole.

In the side of what had seemed to be a snow bank stood a solid-looking little door, painted a dark green. An iron bell-pull hung by the side, and below it, on a small brass plate, neatly engraved in square capital letters, they could read by the aid of moonlight:

MR BADGER.

Saviours of the Train

From *The Railway Children*
by E Nesbit

Their mother was so delighted with the cherries
they had picked for her that they had picked
that the three children racked their brains to think
of some other surprise for her. But all the racking
did not bring out any idea more novel than wild
strawberries. And this idea occurred to them very
next morning.

They had seen the flowers on the plants in the
spring, and they knew where to find wild
strawberries. The plants grew all up and along the

rocky face of the cliff out of which the mouth of the tunnel opened. There were all sorts of trees there – birches and beeches and baby oaks and hazels – and among them the red strawberries glistened on the ground like rubies in the sun.

The mouth of the tunnel was some way from Three Chimneys, so Mother let them take their lunch with them in a basket. And the basket would do to bring the strawberries back in if they found any. She also lent them her silver watch so that they should not be late home for tea – Peter's Waterbury had taken it into its head not to go since the day when Peter dropped it into the water-butt. And they started.

When they reached the very the top of the cutting, they leant over the fence and looked down to where the railway lines lay at the bottom of what, as Phyllis said, looked exactly like a mountain gorge.

"If it wasn't for the railway at the bottom, it

would be as though the foot of man had never been there, wouldn't it?" she said.

The sides of the cutting were of grey stone, very roughly hewn. Indeed the top part of the cutting

had been a little natural glen that had been cut deeper to bring it down to the level of the tunnel's mouth. Among the rocks, grass and wild flowers grew, and seeds dropped by birds in the crannies of the stone had taken root and grown into bushes and trees that overhung the cutting. Near the tunnel was a flight of steps leading down to the line – no more than wooden bars roughly fixed into the earth – a very steep, narrow way up and down, more like a ladder than a stair.

"We'd better get down," said Peter; "I'm sure the strawberries would be quite easy to get at from the side of the steps. You remember it was there we picked the cherry blossoms that we put on the rabbit's funeral grave."

So they went along the fence towards the little swing gate that is at the top of these steps. And they were almost at the gate when Bobbie said: "Hush. Stop! What's that?"

'That' was a very odd noise indeed – a soft noise,

but quite plainly to be heard through the sound of the wind in the tree branches, and the hum and whirr of the telegraph wires. It was a sort of rustling, whispering sound. As they listened it stopped, and then it began again.

And this time it did not stop, but it grew louder and more rustling and rumbling. "Look," cried Peter, suddenly; "the tree over there!"

The tree he pointed at was one of those that have rough grey leaves and white flowers. The berries, when they come, are bright scarlet, but if you pick them, they disappoint you by turning black before you get them home. And, as Peter pointed, they all saw that the tree was moving – but not just the way that trees ought to move when the wind blows through them, but all in one piece, as though it were a live creature and were walking down the side of the cutting.

"It's moving!" cried Bobbie. "Oh, look! And so are the others. It's like the woods in Macbeth."

"It's magic," said Phyllis, breathlessly. "I always knew this railway was enchanted."

It really did seem a little like magic. For all the trees for about twenty yards of the opposite bank seemed to be slowly walking down towards the railway line, the tree with the grey leaves bringing up the rear like some old shepherd driving a flock of green sheep.

"What is it? Oh, what is it?" said Phyllis; "it's much too magic for me. I don't like it. We should go home."

But Bobby and Peter clung fast to the rail and watched breathlessly. And Phyllis made no movement towards going home by herself.

The trees moved on and on. Some stones and loose earth fell down and rattled on the railway metals far below.

"It's all coming down," Peter tried to say, but he found there was hardly any voice to say it with.

And, indeed, just as he spoke, the great rock, on

the top of which the walking trees were, all leant slowly forward. The trees, ceasing to walk, stood still and shivered. Leaning with the rock, they seemed to hesitate a moment, and then rock and trees and grass and bushes, with a rushing sound, slipped right away from the face of the cutting and fell on the line with a blundering crash that could have been heard half a mile off. A cloud of dust rose up.

"Oh," said Peter, in awestruck tones, "isn't it exactly like when coals come in? If there wasn't any roof to the cellar and you could see down."

"Look what a great mound it's made!" said Bobbie.

"Yes, it's all gone right across the down line," said Phyllis.

"That'll take some sweeping up," said Bobbie.

"Yes," said Peter, slowly. He was still leaning on the fence. "Yes," he said again, still more slowly.

Then he stood upright. "The 11.29 hasn't gone

by yet. We must let them know at the station, or there'll be a most frightful accident."

"Let's run," said Bobbie, and began.

But Peter cried, "Come back!" and looked at Mother's watch. He was very prompt and businesslike, and his face looked whiter than they had ever seen it.

"No time," he said; "it's two miles away, and it's past eleven."

"Couldn't we," suggested Phyllis, breathlessly, "couldn't we all climb up a telegraph post and do something to the wires?"

"We don't know how to," said Peter.

"They do it in war," said Phyllis; "I know I've heard of it."

"They only cut them, silly," said Peter, "and that doesn't do any good. And we couldn't cut

280

them even if we got up, and we couldn't get up. If we had anything red, we could get down on the line and wave it."

"But the train wouldn't see us till it got round the corner, and then it could see the mound just as well as us," said Phyllis. "Better, because it's much bigger than us."

"But if we only had something red," Peter repeated, "we could go round the corner and wave to the train."

"We might wave, anyway."

"They'd only think it was just us, as usual. We've waved so often before. Anyway, let's get down."

They got down the steep stairs as quickly as they could. Bobbie was pale and shivering. Peter's face looked thinner than usual. Phyllis was red-faced and damp with anxiety.

"Oh, how hot I am!" she said; "and I thought it was going to be cold. I wish we hadn't put on our—" she stopped short, and then ended in quite a different tone "our flannel petticoats."

Bobbie turned at the bottom of the stairs. "Oh, yes," she cried. "They're red! Let's take them off."

They did, and with the petticoats rolled up under their arms, ran along the railway, skirting the newly fallen mound of stones and rock and earth, and bent, crushed, twisted trees. They ran at their best pace. Peter led, but the girls were not far behind. They reached the corner that hid the mound from the straight line of railway that ran half a mile without curve or corner.

"Now," said Peter, taking hold of the largest flannel petticoat.

"You're not—" Phyllis faltered, "you're not going to tear them?"

"Shut up," said Peter, with brief sternness.

"Oh, yes," said Bobbie, "tear them into little bits if you like. Don't you see, Phil, if we can't stop the train, there'll be a real live accident, with people killed. Oh, horrible! Here, Peter, you'll never tear it through the band!"

She took the red flannel petticoat from him and tore it off an inch from the band. Then she tore the other in the same way.

"There!" said Peter, tearing in his turn. He divided each petticoat into three pieces. "Now, we've got six flags." He looked at the watch again. "And we've got seven minutes left. We must have flag-staffs."

The knives given to boys are, for some odd reason, seldom of the kind of steel that keeps sharp. The young saplings had to be broken off. Two of them came up by the roots. The leaves were stripped from them.

"We must cut holes in the flags, and run the sticks through the holes," said Peter. And the holes were cut. The knife was sharp enough to cut flannel with. Two of the flags were set up in heaps of loose stones between the sleepers of the down line.

Then Phyllis and Bobbie each took a flag, and

stood poised, ready to wave it as soon as the train came in sight.

"I shall have the other two myself," said Peter, "because it was my idea to wave something red."

"They're our petticoats, though," Phyllis was beginning, but Bobbie interrupted:

"Oh, what does it matter who waves what, if we can only save the train?"

Perhaps Peter had not rightly calculated the number of minutes it would take the 11.29 to get from the station to the place where they were, or perhaps the train was late. Anyway, it seemed a very long time that they waited.

Phyllis grew impatient. "I expect the watch is wrong, and the train's gone by," said she.

Peter relaxed the heroic attitude he had chosen to show off his two flags with. And Bobbie began to feel sick with suspense.

It seemed to her that they had been standing there for hours and hours, holding those silly little red flannel flags that no one would ever notice. The train wouldn't care. It would just go rushing by them and tear round the corner and go crashing into that awful mound. And everyone on it would be killed.

Her hands grew very cold and trembled so that she could hardly hold the flag. And then came the distant rumble and hum of the metals, and a puff of white steam showed far away along the stretch of line.

"Stand firm," said Peter, "and wave like mad! When it gets to that big furze bush step back, but go on waving! Don't stand on the line, Bobbie!"

The train came rattling along very, very fast.

"They don't see us! They won't see us! It's all no good!" cried Bobbie.

The two little flags on the line swayed as the nearing train shook and loosened the heaps of loose stones that held them up. One of them slowly leant over and fell on the line. Bobbie jumped forward and caught it up, and waved it; her hands did not tremble now.

"Keep off the line, you silly cuckoo!" hissed Peter, fiercely.

It seemed that the train came on as fast as ever. It was very near now.

"It's no good," Bobbie said again.

"Stand back!" cried Peter, suddenly, and he dragged Phyllis back by the arm.

But Bobbie cried, "Not yet, not yet!" and waved her two flags right over the line. The front of the engine looked black and enormous. It's voice was loud and harsh.

"Oh, stop, stop, stop!" cried Bobbie. No one heard her. At least Peter and Phyllis didn't, for the oncoming rush of the train covered the sound of her voice with a mountain of sound. But afterwards she used to wonder whether the engine itself had not heard her. It seemed almost as though it had, for it slackened swiftly, slackened and stopped, not

twenty yards from the place where Bobbie's two flags waved over the line. She saw the great black engine stop dead, but somehow she could not stop waving the flags.

And when the driver and the fireman had got off the engine and Peter and Phyllis had gone to meet them and pour out their excited tale of the awful mound just round the corner, Bobbie still waved the flags but more and more feebly and jerkily.

When the others turned towards her she was lying across the line with her hands flung forward and still holding tight to the sticks of the little red flannel flags.

The engine-driver picked her up, carried her to the train, and laid her gently on the cushions of a first-class carriage.

"Gone right off in a faint," he said, " Poor little woman. And no wonder. I'll just 'ave a look at this 'ere mound of yours, and then we'll run you back to the station and get her seen to."

It was horrible to see Bobbie lying so white and
quiet, with her lips blue, and parted.

"I believe that's what people look like when
they're dead," whispered Phyllis.

"Don't!" said Peter, sharply.

They sat by Bobbie on the blue cushions, and the
train ran back. Before it reached their station
Bobbie had sighed and opened her eyes, and rolled
herself over and begun to cry. This cheered the
others wonderfully. They had seen her cry before,
but they had never seen her faint. They had not
known what to do when she was fainting, but now
she was only crying they could thump her on the
back and tell her not to, just as they always did. And
presently, when she stopped crying, they were able
to laugh at her for being such a coward as to faint.

When the station was reached, the three were
the heroes of an agitated meeting on the platform.

The praises they got for their 'prompt action,'
their 'common sense,' their 'ingenuity,' were enough

to have turned anybody's head. Phyllis enjoyed herself thoroughly. She had never been a real heroine before, and the feeling was delicious. Peter's ears got very red. Yet he, too, enjoyed himself. Only Bobbie wished fervently that they all wouldn't. She wanted to get away.

"You'll hear from the Company about this, I expect," said the Station Master.

Bobbie wished she might never hear of it again. She pulled at Peter's jacket.

"Oh, come away, come away! I want to go home," she said.

So they went. And as they went Station Master and Porter and guards and driver and fireman and passengers sent up a cheer.

"Oh, listen," cried Phyllis; "that's for us!"

"Yes," said Peter, "I say, I am glad I thought about something red, and waving it."

"How lucky we did put on our red flannel petticoats!" said Phyllis.

Bobbie said nothing. She could think only of the horrible mound, and the trustful train rushing towards it at full speed.

"And it was us that saved them," said Peter.

"How dreadful if they'd all been killed!" said Phyllis, with enjoyment; "Wouldn't it, Bobbie?"

"We never got any strawberries, after all," said Bobbie, faintly.

The others thought her rather heartless.

MUCH
MISCHIEF

A Mad Tea-party

From *Alice's Adventures in Wonderland*
by Lewis Carroll

There was a table set out under a tree in front of the house, and the March Hare and the Hatter were having tea at it.

A Dormouse was sitting between them, fast asleep, and the other two were using it as a cushion, resting their elbows on it, and talking over its head. 'Very uncomfortable for the Dormouse,' thought Alice; 'only, as it's asleep, I suppose it doesn't mind.'

The table was a large one, but the three were all crowded together at one corner of it: "No room!

A Mad Tea-party

No room!" they cried when they saw Alice coming.

"There's plenty of room!" said Alice indignantly, and she sat down in a large armchair at one end of the table.

"Have some wine," the March Hare said in an encouraging tone.

Alice looked all round the table, but there was nothing on it to drink but tea. "I don't see any wine," she remarked.

"There isn't any," said the March Hare.

"Then it wasn't very civil of you to offer it," said Alice angrily.

"It wasn't very civil of you to sit down without being invited," said the March Hare.

"I didn't know it was your table," said Alice; "it's laid for a great many more than three."

"Your hair wants cutting," said the Hatter. He had been looking at Alice for some time with great curiosity, and this was his first speech.

"You should learn not to make personal

remarks," Alice said with some severity; "it's rude."

The Hatter opened his eyes very wide on hearing this; but all he said was, "Why is a raven like a writing-desk?"

'Come, we shall have some fun now!' thought Alice. 'I'm glad they've begun asking riddles.'

"I believe I can guess that," she added aloud.

"Do you mean that you believe that you can find out the answer to it?" said the March Hare.

"Exactly so," said Alice.

"Then you should say what you mean," the March Hare went on.

"I do," Alice hastily replied; "at least – at least I mean what I say – that's the same thing, you know."

"Not the same thing a bit!" said the Hatter. "You might just as well say that 'I see what I eat' is the same thing as 'I eat what I see'!"

"You might just as well say," added the March Hare, "that 'I like what I get' is the same thing as 'I get what I like'!"

A Mad Tea-party

"You might just as well say," added the Dormouse, who seemed to be talking in his sleep, "that 'I breathe when I sleep' is the same thing as 'I sleep when I breathe'!"

"It is the same thing with you," said the Hatter, and here the conversation dropped, and the party sat silent for a minute, while Alice thought over all she could remember about ravens and writing desks, which wasn't much.

The Hatter was the first to break the silence.

"What day of the month is it?" he said, turning to Alice – he had taken his watch out of his pocket, and was looking at it uneasily, shaking it every now and then, and holding it to his ear.

Alice considered for a while, and then said "The fourth."

"Two days wrong!" sighed the Hatter. "I told you butter wouldn't suit the works!" he added looking angrily at the March Hare.

"It was the best butter," the March Hare meekly replied.

"Yes, but some crumbs must have got in as well," the Hatter grumbled, "you shouldn't have put it in with the bread knife."

The March Hare took the watch and looked at it gloomily. Then he dipped it into his cup of tea, and looked at it again; but he could think of nothing better to say than his first remark, "It was the best butter, you know."

Alice had been looking over his shoulder with some curiosity. "What a funny watch!" she remarked. "It tells the day of the month, and doesn't tell what o'clock it is!"

"Why should it?" muttered the Hatter. "Does

your watch tell you what year it is?"

"Of course not," Alice replied very readily: "but that's because it stays the same year for such a long time together."

"Which is just the case with mine," said the Hatter, triumphantly.

Alice felt dreadfully puzzled. The Hatter's remark seemed to have no sort of meaning in it, and yet it was certainly English.

"I don't quite understand you," she said, as politely as she could.

"The Dormouse is asleep again," said the Hatter, and he poured a little hot tea upon its nose.

The Dormouse shook its head impatiently and said, without opening its eyes, "Of course, of course; just what I was going to remark myself."

"Have you guessed the riddle yet?" the Hatter said, turning to Alice again.

"No, I must give it up," Alice replied. "What's the answer?"

"I haven't the slightest idea," said the Hatter.

"Nor I," said the March Hare.

Alice sighed wearily. "I think you might do something better with the time," she said, "than waste it in asking riddles that have no answers."

"If you knew Time as well as I do," said the Hatter, "you wouldn't talk of wasting it. It's him."

"I don't know what you mean," said Alice.

"Of course you don't!" the Hatter said, tossing his head contemptuously. "I dare say you never even spoke to Time!"

"Perhaps not," Alice cautiously replied: "but I know I have to beat time when I learn music."

"Ah! that accounts for it," said the Hatter. "He won't stand beating. Now, if you only kept on good terms with him, he'd do almost anything you liked with the clock. For instance, suppose it were nine o'clock in the morning, just time to begin lessons: you'd only have to whisper a hint to Time, and round goes the clock in a twinkling! Half past one, time for dinner!"

"I only wish it was," the March Hare said to itself in a whisper.

"That would be grand, certainly," said Alice thoughtfully; "but then I shouldn't be hungry for it, you know."

"Not at first, perhaps," said the Hatter: "but you could keep it to half past one as long as you liked."

"Is that the way you manage?" Alice asked.

The Hatter shook his head mournfully. "Not I!" he replied. "We quarrelled last March – just before he went mad, you know," (pointing with his tea spoon at the March Hare) " – it was at the great concert given by the Queen of Hearts, and I had to sing 'Twinkle, twinkle, little bat! How I wonder what you're at!' You know the song, perhaps?"

"I've heard something like it," said Alice.

"It goes on, you know," the Hatter continued, "in this way:

'Up above the world you fly, Like a tea tray in the

sky. Twinkle, twinkle—'"

Here the Dormouse shook itself, and began singing in its sleep, "Twinkle, twinkle, twinkle, twinkle..." and went on so long that they had to pinch it to make it stop.

"Well, I'd hardly reached the end of the first verse," said the Hatter, "when the Queen jumped up and bawled out, 'He's murdering the time! Off with his head!'"

"How dreadfully savage!" exclaimed Alice.

"And ever since that," the Hatter went on in a mournful tone, "he won't do a thing I ask! It's always six o'clock now."

A bright idea came into Alice's head. "Is that the reason so many tea things have been put out here?" she asked.

"Yes, that's it," said the Hatter with a sigh: "it's always teatime, and we've no time to wash the things between whiles."

"Then you must keep moving round, I suppose?" said Alice.

"Exactly so," said the Hatter; "as the things get used up."

"But what happens when you come to the beginning again?" Alice ventured to ask.

"Suppose we change the subject," the March Hare interrupted, yawning. "I'm getting tired of this. I vote the young lady tells us a story."

"I'm afraid I don't know one," said Alice, rather alarmed at the proposal.

"Then the Dormouse shall!" they both cried. "Wake up, Dormouse!" And they pinched it on both sides at once.

The Dormouse slowly opened his eyes.

"I wasn't asleep," he said in a hoarse, feeble voice. "I heard every word you fellows were saying."

"Tell us a story!" said the March Hare.

"Yes, please do!" pleaded Alice.

"And be quick about it," added the Hatter, "or you'll be asleep again before it's done."

"Once upon a time there were three little sisters," the Dormouse began in a great hurry; "and their names were Elsie, Lacie, and Tillie; and they lived at the bottom of a well—"

"What did they live on?" said Alice, who always took a great interest in questions of eating and drinking.

"They lived on treacle," said the Dormouse, after thinking a minute or two.

"They couldn't have done that, you know," Alice

gently remarked; "they'd have been ill."

"So they were," said the Dormouse; "very ill."

Alice tried to fancy to herself what such an extraordinary way of living would be like, but it puzzled her too much, so she went on: "But why did they live at the bottom of a well?"

"Take some more tea," the March Hare said to Alice, very earnestly.

"I've had nothing yet," Alice replied in an offended tone, "so I can't take more."

"You mean you can't take less," said the Hatter: "it's very easy to take more than nothing."

"Nobody asked your opinion," said Alice.

"Who's making personal remarks now?" the Hatter asked triumphantly.

Alice did not quite know what to say to this, so she helped herself to some tea and bread and butter, and then turned back to the Dormouse, and repeated her question. "Why did they live at the bottom of a well?"

The Dormouse again took a minute or two to think about it, and then said, "It was a treacle-well."

"There's no such thing!" Alice was beginning very angrily, but the Hatter and the March Hare went "Sh! sh!" and the Dormouse sulkily remarked, "If you can't be civil, you had better finish the story for yourself."

"No, please go on!" Alice said very humbly; "I won't interrupt again. I dare say there may be one."

"One, indeed!" said the Dormouse indignantly. However, he consented to go on. "And so these three little sisters – they were learning to draw, you know—"

"What did they draw?" said Alice, quite forgetting her promise.

"Treacle," said the Dormouse, without considering at all this time.

"I want a clean cup," interrupted the Hatter. "Let's all move one place on."

He moved on as he spoke, and the Dormouse

followed him: the March Hare moved into the Dormouse's place, and Alice rather unwillingly took the place of the March Hare. The Hatter was the only one who got any advantage from the change, and Alice was a good deal worse off than before, as the March Hare had just upset the milk jug into his plate.

Alice did not wish to offend the Dormouse again, so she began again very cautiously: "But I don't think I understand. Where did they draw the treacle from?"

"You can draw water out of a water well," said the Hatter; "so I should think you could draw treacle out of a treacle well – eh, stupid?"

"But they were in the well," Alice said to the Dormouse, not choosing to notice this last remark.

"Well, of course they were," said the Dormouse. "Well in."

This answer so confused poor Alice, that she let the Dormouse go on for some time without interrupting it.

"They were learning to draw," the Dormouse went on, yawning and rubbing its eyes, for it was getting very sleepy; "and they drew all manner of things – everything that begins with an 'M'—"

"Why with an 'M'?" said Alice.

"Why not?" said the March Hare.

Alice was silent.

The Dormouse had closed its eyes by this time, and was going off into a doze; but, on being pinched by the Hatter, it woke up again with a little shriek, and went on: "—that begins with an 'M', such as mousetraps, and the moon, and memory, and muchness – you know you say things are 'much of a muchness' – did you ever see such a thing as a drawing of a muchness?"

"Really, now you ask me," said Alice, very much confused, "I don't think—"

"Then you shouldn't talk," said the Hatter.

This piece of rudeness was more than Alice

A Mad Tea-party

could bear: she got up in great disgust, and walked off. The Dormouse fell asleep instantly, and neither of the others took the least notice of her going, though she looked back once or twice, half hoping that they would call after her. The last she saw of them, they were trying to put the Dormouse into the teapot.

"At any rate I'll never go there again!" said Alice as she picked her way through the wood. "It's the stupidest tea-party I ever was at in all my life!"

Just as she said this, she noticed that one of the trees had a door leading right into it. 'That's very curious!' she thought.

I've so wanted to sleep in the same room with someone, sometime – someone that belonged to me, you know; not a Ladies' Aider. I've had them. My! I reckon I am glad now those screens didn't come! Wouldn't you be?"

There was no reply. Miss Polly was stalking on ahead. Miss Polly, to tell the truth, was feeling curiously helpless. For the third time since Pollyanna's arrival, Miss Polly had been trying to punish Pollyanna, and for the third time she was being confronted with the amazing fact that her punishment was being taken as some kind of special reward of merit. No wonder Miss Polly was feeling curiously helpless.

Wool and Water

From *Through the Looking-glass*
by Lewis Carroll

Alice looked at the Queen as her voice rose to a squeak. "Much be-etter! Be-etter! Be-e-e-etter! Be-e-ehh!" The last word ended in a long bleat, so like a sheep that Alice quite started.

She looked at the Queen, who seemed to have suddenly wrapped herself up in wool. Alice rubbed her eyes, and looked again. She couldn't make out what had happened at all. Was she in a shop? And was that really – was it really a sheep that was sitting on the other side of the counter? Rub as she could, she could make nothing more of it. She was in a little dark shop, leaning with her elbows on the counter, and opposite to her was an old sheep, sitting in an arm-chair knitting, and every now and then leaving off to look at her through a great pair of spectacles.

"What is it you want to buy?" the sheep said at last, looking up for a moment from her knitting.

"I don't quite know yet," Alice said, very gently. "I should like to look all round me first, if I might."

"You may look in front of you, and on both sides, if you like," said the sheep: "but you can't look all round you – unless you've got eyes at the back of your head."

But these, as it happened, Alice had not got, so she contented herself with turning round, looking at the shelves as she came to them.

The shop seemed to be full of all manner of curious things – but the oddest part of it all was, that whenever she looked hard at any shelf, to make

out exactly what it had on it, that particular shelf was always quite empty, though the others round it were crowded as full as they could hold.

"Things flow about so here!" she said at last in a plaintive tone, after she had spent a minute or so vainly pursuing a large bright thing, that looked sometimes like a doll and sometimes like a work-box, and was always in the shelf next above the one she was looking at. "And this one is the most provoking of all – but I'll tell you what—" she added, as a sudden thought struck her, "I'll follow it up to the very top shelf of all. It'll puzzle it to go through the ceiling, I expect!"

But even this plan failed: the 'thing' went through the ceiling as quietly as possible, as if it were quite used to it.

"Are you a child or a teetotum?" the sheep said, as she took up another pair of needles. "You'll make me giddy soon, if you go on turning round and round like that." She was now working with fourteen pairs at once, and Alice couldn't help looking at her in great astonishment.

'How can she knit with so many?' the puzzled child thought to herself. 'She gets more and more like a porcupine every minute!'

"Can you row?" the sheep asked, handing her a pair of knitting-needles as she spoke.

"Yes, a little. But not on land – and not with needles—" Alice was beginning to say, when suddenly the needles turned into oars in her hands, and she found they were in a little boat, gliding along between banks, so there was nothing for it but to do her best.

"Feather!" cried the sheep, as she took up another pair of needles.

This didn't sound like a remark that needed any answer, so Alice said nothing, but pulled away. There was something very queer about the water, she thought, as every now and then the oars got fast in it, and would hardly come out again.

"Feather! Feather!" the sheep cried again, taking more needles. "You'll be catching a crab directly."

'A dear little crab!' thought Alice to herself. 'I should like that.'

"Didn't you hear me say 'Feather'?" the sheep cried angrily, taking up quite a bunch of needles.

"Indeed I did," said Alice: "you've said it very often – and very loud. Please, where are the crabs?"

"In the water, of course!" said the sheep, sticking some of the needles into her hair, as her hands were full. "Feather, I say!"

"Why do you say 'feather' so often?" Alice asked at last, rather vexed. "I'm not a bird!"

"You are," said the sheep: "you're a little goose."

This offended Alice a little, so there was no more conversation for a minute, while the boat glided gently on, sometimes among beds of weeds (which made the oars stick fast in the water, worse than ever), and sometimes under trees, but always with the same tall river-banks frowning over their heads.

"Oh, please! There are some scented rushes!" Alice cried in a sudden transport of delight. "There really are – and such beauties!"

"You needn't say 'please' to me about 'em" the sheep said, without looking up from her knitting: "I didn't put 'em there, and I'm not going to take 'em away."

"No, but I meant – please, may we wait and pick some?" Alice pleaded. "If you don't mind stopping the boat for a minute."

"How am I to stop it?" said the sheep. "If you leave off rowing, it'll stop of itself."

So the boat was left to drift down the stream as it would, till it glided gently in among the waving rushes. And then the little sleeves were carefully rolled up, and the little arms were plunged in elbow-deep to get the rushes a good long way down before breaking them off – and for a while Alice forgot all about the sheep and the knitting, as she bent over the side of the boat, with just the ends of her tangled hair dipping into the water, while with bright eager eyes she caught at one bunch after another of the darling scented rushes.

'I only hope the boat won't tipple over!' she thought to herself. 'Oh, what a lovely one! Only I couldn't quite reach it.' And it certainly did seem a little provoking – 'almost as if it happened on purpose,' she thought – that, though she managed to pick plenty of beautiful rushes as the boat glided by, there was always a more lovely one that she couldn't reach.

"The prettiest are always further!" she said at last, with a sigh at the obstinacy of the rushes in growing so far off, as, with flushed cheeks and dripping hair and hands, she scrambled back into her place, and began to arrange her new-found treasures in the boat.

What did it matter to her that the rushes had begun to fade, and to lose all their scent and beauty, from the very moment that she picked them? Even real scented rushes, you know, last only a very little while – and these, being dream-rushes, melted away almost like snow, as they lay in heaps at her feet – but Alice hardly noticed this, there were so many other curious things to think about.

They hadn't gone much farther before the blade of one of the oars got fast in the water and wouldn't come out again, and the consequence was that the handle of it caught her under the chin, and, in spite of a series of little shrieks of "Oh, oh, oh!" from poor Alice, it swept her off the seat, and down among the rushes.

However, she wasn't hurt,

and was soon up again. The sheep went on with her
knitting all the while, as if nothing had happened.
"That was a nice crab you caught!" she remarked, as
Alice got back into her place, very relieved to find
herself still in the boat.

"Was it? I didn't see it," said Alice, peeping
cautiously over the side of the boat into the dark
water. "I wish it hadn't let go – I should so like to
see a little crab to take home with me!" But the
sheep only laughed scornfully, and went on with
her knitting.

"Are there many crabs here?" said Alice.

"Crabs, and all sorts of things," said the sheep:
"plenty of choice, only make up your mind. Now,
what do you want to buy?"

"To buy!" Alice echoed in a tone that was half
astonished and half frightened – for the boat, and
the river, had vanished all in a moment, and she was
back again in the little dark shop.

"I should like to buy an egg, please," she said

timidly. "How do you sell them?"

"Fivepence farthing for one – twopence for two," the sheep replied.

"Then two are cheaper than one?" Alice asked, taking out her purse.

"Only you must eat them both, if you buy two," said the sheep.

"Then I'll have one, please," said Alice, as she put the money down on the counter. For she thought to herself, 'They mightn't be at all nice, you know.'

The sheep took the money, and put it away in a box. Then she said "I never put things into people's hands – that would never do – you must get it for yourself." And so saying, she went off to the other end of the shop, and set the egg upright on a shelf.

'I wonder why it wouldn't do?' thought Alice, as she groped her way among the tables and chairs, for the shop was very dark towards the end. 'The egg seems to get further away the more I walk towards it. Let me see, is this a chair? Why, it's got branches,

I declare! How very odd to find trees growing here! And actually here's a little brook! Well, this is the very queerest shop I ever saw!'

So she went on, wondering more and more at every step, as everything turned into a tree the moment she came up to it, and she quite expected the egg to do the same.

The Little Carrs

From *What Katy Did*
by Susan Coolidge

Katy's name was Katy Carr. She lived in the town of Burnet, which wasn't a very big town, but was growing as fast as it knew how. The house she lived in stood on the edge of town. It was a large square house, white, with green blinds, and had a porch in front over which roses and clematis made a thick bower. Four tall locust trees shaded the gravel path that led to the front gate. On one side of the house was an orchard; on the other side were wood piles and barns, and an ice-house. Behind was

MUCH MISCHIEF

a kitchen garden sloping to the south; and behind that a pasture with a brook in it, and butternut trees, and four cows – two red ones, a yellow one with sharp horns tipped with tin, and a dear little white one named Daisy.

There were six of the Carr children – four girls and two boys. Katy, the oldest, was twelve years old; little Phil, the youngest, was four, and the rest fitted in between.

The Little Carrs

Dr Carr, their Papa, was a dear, kind, busy man, who was away from home all day, taking care of sick people. The children hadn't any Mamma. She had died when Phil was a baby, four years before my story began. Katy could remember her pretty well; to the rest she was but a sad, sweet name, spoken on Sunday, and at prayer-times, or when Papa was specially gentle and solemn.

In place of this Mamma, whom they recollected so dimly, there was Aunt Izzie, Papa's sister, who came to take care of them when Mamma went away on that long journey, from which, for so many months, the little ones kept hoping she might return. Aunt Izzie was a small woman, sharp-faced and thin, rather old-looking, and very neat and particular about everything. She meant to be kind to the children, but they puzzled her very much, because they were not a bit like she herself had been when she was a child. Aunt Izzie had been a gentle, tidy little thing, who loved to sit as Curly Locks did, sewing long seams in the parlour, and to have her head patted by older people, and be told that she was a good girl; whereas Katy tore her dress every day, hated sewing, and didn't care a button about being called 'good,' while Clover and Elsie shied off like restless ponies when anyone tried to pat their heads. It was very perplexing to Aunt Izzie, and she found it quite hard to forgive the children for being so 'unaccountable,' and so little like the boys and girls in Sunday-school memoirs, who were the young people she liked best because they always seemed to behave so well, and who she understood most about.

Then Dr Carr was another person who worried her. He wished to have the children hardy and bold, and encouraged climbing and rough plays, in spite of the bumps and ragged clothes that resulted. In fact, there was just one half-hour of the day when Aunt Izzie was really satisfied about her charges, and that was the half-hour before breakfast, when she had made a law that they were all to sit in their little chairs and learn the Bible verse for the day. At this time she looked at them with pleased eyes – they were all so spick and span, and had such nicely-brushed jackets and such neatly combed hair. But the moment the bell rang her comfort was over. From that time on, they were what she called 'not fit to be seen.' The neighbours pitied her very much. They used to count the sixty stiff white pantalette legs hung out to dry every Monday morning, and say to each other what a sight of washing those children made, and what a chore it must be for poor Miss Carr to keep them so nice. But poor Miss Carr didn't think them at all nice; that was the worst of it.

"Clover, go upstairs and wash your hands! Dorry, pick your hat off the floor and hang it on the nail! Not that nail, the third nail from the corner!" These were the kind of things Aunt Izzie was saying all day long. The children minded her pretty well, but they didn't exactly love her, I fear. They called her 'Aunt Izzie' always, never 'Aunty.' Boys and girls will know what that meant.

I want to show you the little Carrs, and I don't know that I could ever have a better chance than one day when five out of the six were perched on top of the ice-house, like chickens on a roost. This ice-house was one of their favourite places. It was only a low roof set over a hole in the ground, and, as it stood in the very middle of the side-yard, it always seemed to the children that the shortest road to every place was to go up one of its slopes and down the other.

They also liked to mount to the ridge-pole, and then, still keeping the sitting position, to let go, and scrape slowly down over the warm shingles to the ground. It was bad for their shoes and trousers, of course; but what of that? Shoes and trousers and clothes generally were Aunt Izzie's affair; theirs was to slide and enjoy themselves.

The Little Carrs

Clover, next in age to Katy, sat at one end. She was a fair, sweet dumpling of a girl, with thick pigtails of light brown hair, and short-sighted blue eyes, which seemed to hold tears, just ready to fall from under the blue. Really, Clover was the jolliest little thing in the world; but these eyes, and her soft cooing voice, always made people feel like petting her and taking her part.

Once, when she was very small, Clover ran away with Katy's doll, and when Katy pursued, and tried to take it back from her, Clover held fast and would not let go. Dr Carr, who wasn't attending particularly, heard nothing but the pathetic tone of Clover's voice, as she said: "Me won't! Me want Dolly!" and, without stopping to inquire, he called out sharply, "For shame, Katy! Give your sister her doll at once!" which Katy, much surprised, did; while Clover purred in triumph, like a satisfied kitten. Clover was sunny and sweet-tempered, a little indolent, and very modest about herself, though, in fact, she was particularly clever in all sorts of games, and extremely droll and funny in a quiet way. Everybody loved her, and she loved everybody, especially Katy, whom she looked up to as one of the wisest people in the world.

Pretty little Phil sat at the other end. Elsie, a thin, brown child of eight, with beautiful dark eyes, and crisp, short curls covering the whole of her small head sat in the very middle.

Poor little Elsie was the 'odd one' among the Carrs. She didn't seem to belong exactly to either the older or the younger children. The great desire and ambition of her heart was to be allowed to go about with Katy and Clover and Cecy Hall, and to know their secrets and be permitted to put notes into the little post-offices they were for ever establishing in all sorts of hidden places. But they didn't want Elsie, and used to tell her to 'run away and play with the children,' which hurt her feelings very much. When she wouldn't run away, I am sorry to say they ran away from her which, as their legs were longest, it was easy to do. Poor Elsie, left behind, would cry bitter tears and, as she was too proud to play much with Dorry and John, her principal comfort was tracking the older ones about and discovering their mysteries, which were her greatest grievance.

Katy, who had the finest plans in the world for being 'heroic' and of use, never saw, as she drifted on her heedless way, that here, in this lonely little sister, was the very chance she wanted for being a comfort to somebody who needed comfort very much. And Elsie's heavy heart went uncheered.

Dorry and Joanna sat on either side of Elsie.

Dorry was six years old; a pale, pudgy boy, with rather a solemn face, and smears of molasses on the sleeve of his jacket. Joanna, whom the children called 'John,' and 'Johnnie,' was a square, splendid child, a year younger than Dorry; she had big brave eyes, and a wide rosy mouth, which always looked ready to laugh. These two were great friends, though Dorry seemed like a girl who had got into boy's clothes by mistake, and Johnnie like a boy who, in a fit of fun, had borrowed his sister's frock.

And now, as they all sat there chattering and giggling, the window in the house above opened, a glad shriek was heard, and Katy's head appeared. In her hand she held a heap of stockings, which she waved triumphantly.

"Hurray!" she cried, "all done, and Aunt Izzie says we may go. Are you tired out waiting? I couldn't help it, the holes were so big, and took so long. Hurry up, Clover, and get the things! Cecy and I will be down in a minute."

The Little Carrs

The children all jumped up gladly at once, and slid down the roof. Clover fetched a couple of baskets from the wood shed. Elsie ran for her kitten. Dorry and John loaded themselves with two great bundles of green boughs. Just as they were ready the side-door banged, and Katy and Cecy Hall came into the yard.

I must tell you about Cecy. She was a great friend of the children's, and lived in the house next door. The yards of the houses were only separated by a green hedge with no gate, so that Cecy spent two-thirds of her time at Dr Carr's, and was exactly like one of the family. She was a neat, dapper, pink-and-white girl, modest and prim in manner, with light shiny hair, which always kept smooth, and slim hands, which never looked dirty. How different from my poor Katy! Katy's hair was forever in a snarl, her gowns were always catching on nails and 'tearing themselves' and – in spite of her age and size – she was as heedless and innocent as a child of six. Katy was the longest girl that was ever seen. What she did to make herself grow so, nobody could tell; but there she was – up above Papa's ear and half a head taller than poor Aunt Izzie. Whenever she stopped to think about her height she became very awkward, and felt as if she were all legs and elbows and angles and joints. Happily, her head was so full of other things – of plans and schemes and fancies of all sorts – that she didn't often take time to remember how tall she was.

She was a dear, loving child, for all her careless habits, and made bushels of good resolutions every week of her life, only unluckily she never kept any of them. She had fits of responsibility about the other children, and longed to set them a good example, but when the chance came she generally forgot to do so.

Katy's days flew like the wind; for when she wasn't studying lessons, or sewing and darning with Aunt Izzie (which she hated extremely) there were always so many delightful schemes rioting in her brains, that all she wished for was ten pairs of hands to carry them out.

These same active brains got her into perpetual scrapes. She was fond of building castles in the air, and dreaming of the time when something she had done would make her famous so that everybody would hear of her and want to know her. I don't think she had made up her mind what this wonderful thing was to be; but while thinking about it she often forgot to learn a lesson, or to lace her boots, and then she had a bad mark, or a scolding from Aunt Izzie. At such times she consoled herself with planning how, by and by, she would be beautiful and beloved, and as amiable as an angel.

A great deal was to happen to Katy before that time came. Her eyes, which were black, were to turn blue; her nose was to lengthen and straighten, and her mouth – quite too large at present to suit the part of a heroine – was to be made over into a sort of rosy button. Meantime, and until these charming changes should take place, Katy forgot her features as much as she could, though still, I think, the person on earth whom she most envied was those ladies on the outsides of the shampoo bottles with the wonderful hair that sweeps the ground.

Golden Guineas

From *Five Children and It*
by E Nesbit

*Five children are staying in the country while their parents are away.
They discover a 'sand-fairy' (the Psammead), who is brown and hairy
with bat's ears and snail's eyes, and seems to be permanently grumpy.
He grants them daily wishes which are quite often disastrous but
which are fortunately unmade at sunset.*

Anthea woke in the morning from a very real sort of dream, in which she was walking in the Zoological Gardens on a pouring wet day without any umbrella. The animals seemed desperately unhappy because of the rain, and were all growling gloomily. When she awoke, both the growling and the rain went on just the same. The growling was the heavy regular breathing of her sister Jane, who had a slight cold and was still asleep. The rain fell in slow drops onto Anthea's face from the wet corner of a towel which her brother Robert was gently squeezing the water out of, to wake her up, as he now explained.

"Oh, drop it!" she said rather crossly; so he did, for he was not a brutal brother, though very ingenious in apple-pie beds, booby-traps, original methods of awakening sleeping relatives, and all those other little accomplishments which made home happy.

"I had such a funny dream," Anthea began.

"So did I," said Jane, wakening suddenly and without warning. "I dreamed we found a Sand-fairy in the gravel-pits, and it said it was a Psammead, and we might have a new wish every day, and—"

"But that's what I dreamed," said Robert; "I was just going to tell you – and we had the first wish directly it said so. And I dreamed you girls were donkeys enough to ask for us all to be beautiful as the day, and we jolly well were, and of course it was perfectly beastly."

"But can different people all dream the same thing?" said Anthea, sitting up in bed, "because I dreamed all that as well as about the Zoo and the rain. And Baby didn't know us in my dream, and the servants shut us out of the house because the radiantness of our beauty was such a complete disguise, and—"

The voice of the eldest brother sounded from across the landing. "Come on Robert," it said, "you'll be late for breakfast again – unless you mean to shirk your bath like you did on Tuesday."

"I say, come here a sec," Robert replied. "I didn't shirk it; I had it after brekker in father's dressing-room, because ours was emptied away."

Cyril appeared in the doorway, partially clothed.

"Look here," said Anthea, "we've all had such an odd dream. We've all dreamed that we found a Sand-fairy."

Her voice died away before Cyril's contemptuous glance. "Dream?" he said; "You little sillies, it's true. I tell you it all happened. That's why I'm so keen on being down early. We'll go up there directly after brekker, and have another wish. Only we'll make up our minds, solid, before we go, what it is we want, and no one must ask for anything unless the others agree first. No more peerless beauties for this child, thank you. Not if I know it!"

The other three dressed, with their mouths open. If all that dream about the Sand-fairy was real, this real dressing seemed very like a dream, the girls thought. Jane felt that Cyril was right, but Anthea was not sure, till after they had seen Martha and heard her full and plain reminders about their naughty conduct the day before. Then Anthea was sure. "Because," said she, "servants never dream anything but the things in dream-books, like snakes and oysters and going to a wedding – that means a funeral, and snakes are a false female friend, and oysters are babies."

"Talking of babies," said Cyril, "where's the Lamb got to?"

"Martha's going to take him to Rochester to see her cousins. Mother said she might. She's dressing him now," said Jane, "in his very best coat and hat. Bread and butter, please."

"She seems to like taking him too," said Robert in a tone of wonder.

"Servants do like taking babies to see their relations," Cyril said; "I've noticed it before –

especially in their best things."

"I expect they pretend they're their own babies, and that they're not servants at all, but married to noble dukes of high degree, and they say the babies are the little dukes and duchesses," Jane suggested dreamily, taking more marmalade. "I expect that's what Martha'll say to her cousin. She'll enjoy herself most frightfully."

"She won't enjoy herself most frightfully carrying our infant duke to Rochester," said Robert; "not if she's anything like me, she won't."

"Fancy walking to Rochester with the Lamb on your back! Oh, crikey!" said Cyril in full agreement.

"She's going by carrier," said Jane. "Let's see them off, then we shall have done a polite and kindly act, and we shall be quite sure we've got rid of them for the day."

So they did. Martha wore her Sunday dress of two shades of purple, so tight in the chest that it made her stoop, and her blue hat with the pink cornflowers and white ribbon. She had a yellow-lace collar with a green bow. And the Lamb had indeed his very best cream-coloured silk coat and hat. It was a smart party that the carrier's cart picked up at the Cross Roads.

When its white tilt and red wheels had slowly vanished in a swirl of chalkdust, Cyril said: "And now for the Psammead!"

And off they went.

As they went they decided on the wish they would ask for. Although they were all in a great hurry they did not try to climb down the sides of the gravel-pit, but went round by the safe lower road, as if they had been carts. They had made a ring of stones round the place where the Sand-fairy had disappeared, so they easily found the spot again. The sun was burning and bright, and the sky was deep blue and without a cloud. The sand was very hot to touch.

"Suppose it was only a dream, after all," Robert

said as the boys uncovered their spades from the sand-heap where they had buried them and began to dig.

"Suppose you were a sensible chap," said Cyril; "one's quite as likely as the other!"

"Suppose you kept a civil tongue in your head," Robert snapped.

"Suppose we girls take a turn," said Jane, laughing. "You boys seem to be getting very warm."

"Suppose you don't come shoving your silly oar in," said Robert, who was now warm indeed.

"We won't," said Anthea quickly. "Robert dear, don't be so grumpy – we won't say a word, you shall be the one to speak to the Fairy and tell him what we've decided to wish for. You'll say it much better than we shall."

"Suppose you drop being a little humbug," said Robert, but not crossly. "Look out – dig with your hands, now!"

So they did, and presently uncovered the

Golden Guineas

spider-shaped brown hairy body, long arms and legs, bat's ears and snail's eyes of the Sand-fairy himself. Everyone drew a deep breath of satisfaction, for now of course it couldn't have been a dream. The Psammead sat up and shook the sand out of its fur.

"How's your left whisker this morning?" said Anthea politely.

"Nothing to boast of," said it; "it had rather a restless night. But thank you for asking."

"I say," said Robert, "do you feel up to giving wishes today, because we very much want an extra besides the regular one? The extra's a very little one," he added reassuringly.

"Humph!" said the Sand-fairy. (If you read this story aloud, please pronounce 'humph' exactly as it is spelt, for that is how he said it.) "Humph! Do you know, until I heard you being disagreeable to each other just over my head, and so loud too, I really quite thought I had dreamed you all. I do have very odd dreams sometimes."

"Do you?" Jane hurried to say, so as to get away from the subject of disagreeableness. "I wish," she added politely, "you'd tell us about your dreams – they must be awfully interesting."

"Is that the day's wish?" asked the Sand-fairy, yawning and closing its eyes.

Cyril muttered something about 'just like a girl,' and the rest stood silent. If they said 'Yes,' then goodbye to the other wishes they had decided to ask for. If they said 'No,' it would be very rude, and they had all been taught manners, and had learnt a little too, which is not at all the same thing. A sigh of relief broke from all lips when the Sand-fairy said: "If I do I shan't have strength to give you a second wish; not even good tempers, or common sense, or manners, or little things like that."

"We don't want you to put yourself out at all about these things, we can manage them quite well ourselves," said Cyril eagerly; while the others looked guiltily at each other, and wished the Fairy would not keep all on about good tempers, but give them one good rowing if it wanted to, and then have done with it.

"Well," said the Psammead, putting out his long snail's eyes so suddenly that one of them nearly went into the round boy's eye of Robert, "let's have the little wish first."

"We don't want the servants to notice the gifts you give us."

"Are kind enough to give us," said Anthea in a whisper.

"Are kind enough to give us, I mean," said Robert, hastily.

The Fairy swelled himself out a bit, let his breath go, and said "I've done that for you – it was quite easy. People don't notice things much, anyway. What's the next wish?"

"We want," said Robert slowly, "to be rich beyond the dreams of something or other."

"Avarice," said Jane.

"So it is," said the Fairy unexpectedly. "But it won't do you much good, that's one comfort," it muttered to itself. "Come – I can't go beyond dreams, you know! How much do you want, and will you have it in gold or notes?"

"Gold, please – and millions of it."

"This gravel-pit full be enough?" said the Fairy in an offhand manner.

"Oh yes!"

"Then get out before I begin, or you'll be buried alive in it."

It made its skinny arms so long, and waved them so frighteningly, that the children ran as hard as they could towards the road by which carts used to come to the gravel-pits. Only Anthea had presence of mind enough to shout a timid "I hope your whisker will be better tomorrow," as she ran.

On the road they turned and looked back, and they had to shut their eyes, and open them very slowly, a little bit at a time, because the sight was too dazzling for their eyes to be able to bear it. It was something like trying to look at the sun at high noon on Midsummer Day. For the whole of the sand-pit was full, right up to the very top, with new shining gold pieces, and all the little sand-martins' little front doors were covered out of sight. Where the road for the carts wound into the gravel-pit the gold lay in heaps like stones lie by the roadside, and a great bank of shining gold shelved down from where it lay flat and smooth between the tall sides of the gravel-pit. And all the gleaming heap was minted gold. And on the sides and edges of these countless coins the midday sun shone and sparkled, and glowed and gleamed till the quarry looked like the mouth of a smelting furnace, or one of the fairy halls that you see sometimes in the sky at sunset.

The children stood with their mouths open, and no one said a word.

At last Robert stooped and picked up one of the loose coins from the edge of the heap by the cart-road, and looked at it. He looked on both sides. Then he said in a low voice, quite different to his own, "It's not sovereigns."

"It's gold, anyway," said Cyril. And now they all began to talk at once. They all picked up the golden treasure by handfuls and let it run through their fingers like water, and the chink it made as it fell was wonderful music. At first they quite forgot to think of spending the money, it was so nice to play with. Jane sat down between two heaps of gold, and Robert began to bury her, as you bury your father in sand when you are at the seaside and he has gone to sleep on the beach with his newspaper over his face.

But Jane was not half buried before she cried out, "Oh, stop, it's too heavy! It hurts!"

Robert said "Bosh!" and went on.

"Let me out, I tell you," cried Jane, and was taken out, very white, and trembling a little.

"You've no idea what it's like," she said; "it's like stones on you – or like chains."

"Look here," Cyril said, "if this is to do us any good, it's no good our staying gasping at it like this. Let's fill our pockets and go and buy things. Don't you forget, it won't last after sunset. I wish we'd asked the Psammead why things don't turn to stone. Perhaps this will. I'll tell you what, there's a pony and cart in the village."

"Do you want to buy that?" asked Jane.

"No, silly – we'll hire it. And then we'll go to Rochester and buy heaps and heaps of things. Look here, let's each take as much as we can carry. But it's not sovereigns. They've got a man's head on one side and a thing like the ace of spades on the other.

Golden Guineas

Fill your pockets with it, I tell you, and come along. You can jaw as we go – if you must jaw."

Cyril sat down and began to fill his pockets. "You all made fun of me for getting father to have nine pockets in my Norfolks," said he, "but now you see!"

They did. For when Cyril had filled his nine pockets and his handkerchief and the space between himself and his shirt front with the gold coins, he had to stand up. But he staggered, and had to sit down again in a hurry.

"Throw out some of the cargo," said Robert. "You'll sink the ship, old chap. That's what comes of nine pockets."

And Cyril had to.

Then they set off to walk to the village. It was more than a mile, and the road was very dusty indeed, and the sun seemed to get hotter and hotter, and the gold coins in their pockets got heavier and heavier.

It was Jane who said, "I don't see how we're to spend it all. There must be thousands of pounds among the lot of us. I'm going to leave some of mine behind this stump in the hedge. And directly we get to the village we'll buy some biscuits – I know it's long past dinner-time." She took out a handful or two of gold and hid it in the hollows of an old hornbeam. "How round and yellow they are," she said. "Don't you wish they were gingerbread nuts and we were going to eat them?"

"Well, they're not, and we're not," said Cyril. "Come on!"

But they came on heavily and wearily. Before they reached the village, more than one stump in the hedge concealed its little hoard of hidden treasure. Yet they reached the village with about twelve hundred guineas in their pockets. But in spite of this inside wealth they looked quite ordinary outside, and no one would have thought they could have more than a half-crown each at the outside. The haze of heat, the blue of the wood smoke, made a sort of dim misty cloud over the red roofs of the village. The four sat down heavily on the first bench they came to. It happened to be outside the Blue Boar Inn.

It was decided that Cyril should go into the Blue Boar and ask for ginger beer, because, as Anthea said, "It is not wrong for men to go into public houses, only for children. And Cyril is nearer to being a man than us, because he is the eldest." So he went. The others sat in the sun and waited.

"Oh, hats, how hot it is!" said Robert. "Dogs put their tongues out when they're hot; I wonder if it would cool us at all to put out ours?"

"We might try," Jane said; and they all put their tongues out as far as they could go, so that it quite stretched their throats, but it only seemed to make them thirstier than ever, besides annoying everyone who went by. So they took their tongues in again, just as Cyril came back with the ginger beer.

"I had to pay for it out of my own two-and-sevenpence, though, that I was going to buy rabbits with," he said. "They wouldn't change the gold. And when I pulled out a handful the man just laughed and said it was card-counters. And I got some sponge cakes too, out of a glass jar on the bar counter. And some biscuits with caraways in."

The sponge-cakes were both soft and dry and the biscuits were dry too, and yet soft, which biscuits ought not to be. But the ginger beer was delicious, and made up for everything.

"It's my turn now to try to buy something with the money," Anthea said; "I'm next eldest. Where is the pony-cart kept?"

It was at The Chequers. Anthea went in the back

364

way to the yard, because they all knew that little girls ought not to go into the bars of public houses.

"He'll be ready in a brace of shakes, he says," she remarked, when she came out. "And he's to have one sovereign – or whatever it is – to drive us in to Rochester and back, besides waiting there till we've got everything we want. I think I managed it all quite well."

"You think yourself jolly clever, I daresay," said Cyril moodily. "How did you do it?"

"I wasn't jolly clever enough to go taking handfuls of money out of my pocket, to make it seem cheap, anyway," she retorted.

"I just found a young man doing something to a horse's leg with a sponge and a pail. And I held out one sovereign, and I said, 'Do you know what this is?' He said, 'No,' and he'd call his father. And the old man came, and he said it was a spade guinea; and he said was it my own to do as I liked with, and I said 'Yes'; and I asked about the pony-cart, and I said he could have the guinea if he'd drive us in to Rochester. And his name is S Crispin. And he said, 'Right oh.'"

It was a new sensation to be driven in a smart pony-trap along pretty country roads; it was very pleasant too (which is not always the case with new sensations), quite apart from the beautiful plans of spending the money that each child made as they went along, silently of course and quite to itself, for they felt it would never have done to let the old innkeeper hear them talk in the affluent sort of way they were thinking in. The old man put them down by the bridge at their request.

"If you were going to buy a carriage and horses, where would you go?" asked Cyril, as if he were only asking for the sake of something to say.

"Billy Peasemarsh, at the Saracen's Head," said the old man promptly. "Though all forbid I should recommend any man where it's a question of horses, no more than I'd take anybody else's recommending if I was a-buying one. But if your pa's thinking of a turnout of any sort, there ain't a straighter man in Rochester, nor a civiller spoken, than Billy, though I says it."

"Thank you," said Cyril. "The Saracen's Head."

And now the children began to see one of the laws of nature turn upside down and stand on its head like an acrobat. Any grown-up person would tell you that money is hard to get and easy to spend. But the fairy money had been easy to get, and spending it was not only hard, it was almost impossible. The tradespeople of Rochester seemed to shrink, to a trades-person, from the glittering fairy gold ('furrin money' they called it, for the most part).

To begin with, Anthea, who had had the misfortune to sit on her hat earlier in the day, wished to buy another. She chose a very beautiful one, trimmed with pink roses and the blue feathers of peacocks. It was sitting in the window, and was marked, 'Paris Model, three guineas.'

"I'm glad," she said, "because, if it says guineas, it means guineas, and not sovereigns, which we haven't got."

But when she took three of the spade guineas in her hand, which was by this time rather dirty owing to her not having put on gloves before going to the gravel-pit, the black-silk young lady in the shop looked very hard at her, and went and whispered something to an older and uglier lady, also in black silk, and then they gave her back the money and said it was not current coin.

"But it's good money," said Anthea, "and it is my own."

"I daresay," said the lady, "but it's not the kind of money that's fashionable now, and we don't care about taking it."

"I believe they think we've stolen it," said Anthea, rejoining the others in the street; "if we at least had gloves they wouldn't think we were so dishonest. It's my hands being so dirty that fills their minds with doubts."

So they chose a humble shop, and the girls bought cotton gloves, the kind at sixpence three-farthings, but when they offered a guinea the woman looked at it through her spectacles and said she had no change; so the gloves had to be paid for out of Cyril's two-and-sevenpence that he meant to buy rabbits with, and so had the green imitation crocodile-skin purse at ninepence-halfpenny which had been bought at the same time. They tried several more shops, the kinds where you buy toys and scent, and silk handkerchiefs and books, and fancy boxes of stationery, and photographs of objects of interest in the vicinity.

But nobody cared to change a guinea that day in Rochester, and as they went from shop to shop they got dirtier and dirtier, and their hair got more and more untidy, and Jane slipped and fell down on a part of the road where a water-cart had just gone by.

Also they got very hungry, but they found no one would give them anything to eat for their guineas. After trying the shops of two pastry-cooks in vain, they became so hungry, perhaps from the smell of the cake in the shops, as Cyril suggested, that they formed a plan of campaign in whispers and carried it out in desperation.

They marched into a third pastry-cook's – Beale his name was – and before the people behind the counter could interfere each child had seized three new penny buns, clapped the three together between its dirty hands, and taken a big bite out of the triple sandwich. Then they stood at bay, with the twelve buns in their hands and their mouths very full indeed. The

shocked pastry-cook bounded round the corner.

"Here," said Cyril, speaking as distinctly as he could, and holding out the guinea he got ready before entering the shop, "pay yourself out of that."

Mr Beale snatched the coin, bit it, and put it into his pocket.

"Off you go," he said, brief and stern like the man in the song.

"But the change?" said Anthea, who had a saving mind.

"Change!" said the man. "I'll change you! Hout you goes; and you may think yourselves lucky I don't send for the police to find out where you got it!"

In the Castle Gardens the millionaires finished the buns, and though the curranty softness of these were delicious, and acted like a charm in raising the spirits of the party, yet even the stoutest heart quailed at the thought of venturing to sound Mr Billy Peasemarsh at the Saracen's Head on the subject of a horse and carriage. The boys would have given up the idea, but Jane was always a hopeful child, and Anthea generally an obstinate one, and it was their earnestness that prevailed.

The whole party, by this time indescribably dirty, therefore betook itself to the Saracen's Head. The yard-method of attack having been successful at The Chequers was tried again here. Mr Peasemarsh was in the yard, and Robert opened the business in these terms: "They tell me you have a lot of horses and carriages to sell."

It had been agreed that Robert should be spokesman, because in books it is always the gentlemen who buy horses, and not ladies, and Cyril had had his go at the Blue Boar.

"They tell you true, young man," said Mr Peasemarsh. He was a long, lean man, with very blue eyes and a tight mouth and narrow lips.

"We should like to buy some from you, please," said Robert politely.

"I daresay you would."

"Will you show us a few, please? So that we can all choose?"

"Who are you a-kidden of?" inquired Mr Billy Peasemarsh. "Was you sent here of a message?"

"I tell you," said Robert, "we want to buy some horses and carriages, and a man told us you were straight and civil spoken, but I shouldn't wonder if he was mistaken."

"Upon my sacred!" said Mr Peasemarsh. "Shall I trot the whole stable out for your Honour's worship to see? Or shall I send round to the Bishop's to see if he's a nag or two to dispose of?"

"Please do," said Robert, "if it's not too much trouble. It would be very kind of you."

Mr Peasemarsh put his hands in his pockets and laughed, and they did not like the way he did it. Then he shouted "Willum!"

A stooping ostler appeared in a stable door.

"Here, Willum, come and look at this 'ere young dook! Wants to buy the whole stud, lock, stock, and bar'l. And ain't got tuppence in his pocket to bless hisself with, I'll go bail!"

Willum's eyes followed his master's pointing thumb with contemptuous interest. "Do'e, for sure?" he said.

But Robert spoke, though both the girls were now pulling at his jacket and begging him to 'come along'. He spoke, and he was very angry; he said: "I'm not a young duke, and I never pretended to be. And as for tuppence – what do you call this?" And before the others could stop him he had pulled out two fat handfuls of shining guineas, and held them out for Mr Peasemarsh to look at. He did look. He snatched one up in his finger and thumb. He bit it, and Jane expected him to say, 'The best horse in my stables is at your service.'

But the others knew better. Still it was a blow,

even to the most desponding, when he said shortly:
"Willum, shut the yard doors," and Willum grinned
and went to shut them.

"Good afternoon," said Robert hastily; "we
shan't buy any of your horses now, whatever you say,
and I hope it'll be a lesson to you." He had seen a
little side gate open, and was moving towards it as
he spoke.

But Billy Peasemarsh put himself in the way.
"Not so fast, you young off-scouring!" he said.
"Willum, fetch the pleece."

Willum went. The children stood huddled
together like frightened sheep, and Mr Peasemarsh
spoke to them till the 'pleece' arrived. He said many
things. Among other things he said: "Nice lot you
are, aren't you, coming tempting honest men with
your guineas!"

"They are guineas," said Cyril boldly.

"Oh, of course we don't know all about that, no
more we don't – oh no – course not! And dragging

little gells into it too. 'Ere – I'll let the gells go if you'll come along to the pleece quiet."

"We won't be let go," said Jane heroically; "not without the boys. It's our money just as much as theirs, you wicked old man."

"Where'd you get it, then?" said the man, softening slightly, which was not at all what the boys expected when Jane began to call names.

Jane cast a silent glance of agony at the others.

"Lost your tongue, eh? Got it fast enough when it's for calling names with. Come, speak up. Where'd you get it?"

"Out of the gravel-pit," said truthful Jane.

"Next article," said the man.

"I tell you we did," Jane said. "There's a fairy there – all over brown fur – with ears like a bat's and eyes like a snail's, and he gives you a wish a day, and they all come true."

"Touched in the head, eh?" said the man in a low voice. "All the more shame to you boys dragging the poor afflicted child into your sinful burglaries."

"She's not mad; it's true," said Anthea. "There is a fairy. If I ever see him again I'll wish for something for you; at least I would if vengeance wasn't wicked – so there!"

"Lor' lumme," said Billy Peasemarsh, "if there ain't another on 'em!"

And now Willum came back, with a spiteful grin on his face, and at his back a policeman, with

whom Mr Peasemarsh spoke long in a hoarse
earnest whisper.

"I daresay you're right," said the policeman at last.
"Anyway, I'll take 'em up on a charge of unlawful
possession, pending inquiries. And the magistrate
will deal with the case. Send the afflicted ones to a
home, as likely as not, and the boys to a
reformatory. Now then, come along, youngsters!
No use making a fuss. You bring the gells along,
Mr Peasemarsh, sir, and I'll shepherd the boys."

Speechless with rage and horror, the four
children were driven along the streets of Rochester.
Tears of anger and shame blinded them, so that
when Robert ran right into a passer-by he did not
recognize her till a well-known voice said, "Well, if
ever I did. Oh, Master Robert, whatever have you
been a-doing of now?"

And another voice, quite as well known, said,
"Panty; want go own Panty!"

They had run into Martha and the baby!

Golden Guineas

Martha behaved admirably. She refused to believe a word of the policeman's story, or of Mr Peasemarsh's either, even when they made Robert turn out his pockets in an archway and show the guineas.

"I don't see nothing," she said. "You've gone out of your senses, you two! There ain't any gold there – only the poor child's hands, all over crock and dirt, and like the very chimbley. Oh, that I should ever see the day!"

And the children thought this very noble of Martha, even if rather wicked, till they remembered how the Fairy had promised that the servants should never notice any of the fairy gifts. So of course Martha couldn't see the gold, and so was only speaking the truth, and that was quite right, of course, but not extra noble.

It was getting dusk when they reached the police station. The policeman told his tale to an inspector, who sat in a large bare room with a thing like a clumsy nursery-fender at one end to put prisoners in. Robert wondered whether it was a cell or a dock.

"Produce the coins, officer," said the inspector.

"Turn out your pockets," said the constable.

Cyril desperately plunged his hands in his pockets, stood still a moment, and then began to laugh – an odd sort of laugh that hurt, and that felt much more like crying. His pockets were empty. So were the pockets of the others. For of course at sunset all the fairy gold had vanished away.

"Turn out your pockets, and stop that noise," said the inspector.

Cyril turned out his pockets, every one of the nine which enriched his Norfolk suit. And every pocket was empty.

"Well!" said the inspector.

"I don't know how they done it – artful little beggars! They walked in front of me the 'ole way, so as for me to keep my eye on them and not to attract a crowd and obstruct the traffic."

"It's very remarkable," said the inspector, frowning.

"If you've quite done a-browbeating of the innocent children," said Martha, "I'll hire a private carriage and we'll drive home to their papa's mansion. You'll hear about this again young man! I told you they hadn't got any gold, when you were pretending to see it in their poor helpless hands. It's early in the day for a constable on duty not to be able to trust his own eyes. As to the other one, the less said the better; he keeps the Saracen's Head, and he knows best what his liquor's like."

"Take them away, for goodness' sake," said the inspector crossly. But as they left the police station he said, "Now then!" to the policeman and Mr Peasemarsh, and he said it twenty times as crossly as he had spoken to Martha.

Martha was as good as her word. She took them home in a grand carriage, because the carrier's cart was gone, and, though she had stood by them so nobly with the police, she was very angry with them for 'trapseing into Rochester,' that none of them dared to mention the man with the pony-cart from the village who was still waiting for them. And so, after one day of boundless wealth, the children found themselves sent to bed in disgrace, and only enriched by two pairs of cotton gloves, an imitation crocodile-skin purse, and twelve penny buns, long since digested.

The thing that troubled them most was the fear that the old gentleman's guinea might have disappeared at sunset with all the rest, so they went down to the village next day to apologize for not meeting him in Rochester, and to see. They found him very friendly. The guinea had not disappeared, and he had bored a hole in it and hung it on his watch-chain.

As for the guinea the baker took, the children felt they could not care whether it had vanished or not, which was not perhaps honest, but on the other hand was not unnatural. But afterwards this preyed on Anthea's mind, and at last she secretly sent twelve stamps by post to 'Mr Beale, Baker, Rochester.' Inside she wrote, 'To pay for the buns.' I hope the guinea did disappear, for that pastry-cook was really not a nice man and besides, penny buns are seven for sixpence in all respectable shops.

The End